Study Guide

for

Thio

Sociology
A Brief Introduction

Fifth Edition

prepared by

Allyn & Bacon

Boston   New York   San Francisco
Mexico City   Montreal   Toronto   London   Madrid   Munich   Paris
Hong Kong   Singapore   Tokyo   Cape Town   Sydney

ISBN 0-205-37250-3

Printed in the United States of America

10 9 8 7 6 5 4   08 07 06 05 04

Table of Contents

Welcome to the World of Sociology!

You are about to embark on a journey in which you will find the keys to understanding the myths and realities of sociology. Designed to be used in conjunction with your lecture program, and your text by Alex Thio, this Study Guide lets you integrate and build on the sociological concepts presented.

In your Study Guide you will find the following:

Learning Objectives

A list of objectives that you should master after reading each chapter.

Key Concepts

A list of key concepts covered in the text to facilitate learning and retention.

ContentSelect Articles

Articles chosen from ContentSelect, Allyn & Bacon's online database of scholarly journals.

Practice Tests

Once you have finished reading and reviewing a chapter in the book, try to answer the practice test questions. The questions will allow you to see how well you have understood the material presented in each chapter. Multiple-choice, true/false, and short answer/essay questions are included.

Flashcards

Used on your own or with the help of a friend, flashcards can help you learn the key terms from the text. A solid understanding of these terms will provide you with a strong foundation from which to think critically and scientifically. Here are some tips for using these flashcards successfully:

- Once you have cut the cards out, shuffle them so you know the definitions of the terms no matter what order the cards are in.
- Test yourself using both sides of the cards. Try reading the definition and identifying the key term it defines.
- On the back of the card write an example that helps to illustrate the term, either from your reading or personal experience.
- After you have worked through the pile of cards a number of times, begin to separate out the cards you know well leaving only the ones you continue to have difficulty with.

Good luck on your journey!

Chapter 1: The Essence of Sociology

Learning Objectives

After reading Chapter 1, the student should be able to:

1. Describe generally how sociologists define and approach the study of human society.
2. Understand the sociological vision of social life and the special insights it offers into human diversity, global social forces and the sociological imagination.
3. Trace the historical development of sociology.
4. Outline and compare the three major perspectives of sociology, including feminist theory, and show how they can work together to analyze complex social issues.
5. Illustrate the three sociological perspectives through the analysis of sports.
6. State and compare sociology's major research methods.
7. Explore one of sociology's frontiers through the technique of deconstruction.
8. Describe how sociology can enrich our lives by helping to change our world.

Key Concepts

class conflict
conflict perspective
content analysis
control group
detached observation
economic globalization
ethnography
experiment
experimental group
feminist theory
functionalist perspective
hypothesis
latent function
macro view
manifest function
mechanical solidarity
micro view
organic solidarity
outsourcing
participation observation

patriarchy
population
random sample
sample
secondary analysis
social consensus
social forces
social integration
social marginality
sociological imagination
sociology
stratified sampling
structured interview
survey
symbolic interactionist perspective
systematic sampling
theoretical perspective
theory
unstructured interview
verstehen

1

Content Select Articles

[Note: The following articles are available to students through ContentSlect, a data base of sociological articles that students can use through purchase of the text. They can be found in the data base by typing in the author's name.]

Title: Durkheim and the Unthought: Some Dilemmas of Modernity.
Author(s): Ramp, William J.
Abstract: Discusses the possibility of examining the sociological theories of Emile Durkheim as an example of what sociologist Michel Foucault termed the modern encounter with the unthought. Scientific scrutiny of the specific unacknowledged genesis of certain universal categories of modern life; Assessment of Durkheimian sociology; Importance to the understanding of ssues including knowledge and certainty in postmodern sociology.

Title: Sociology as a Moral Discourse: a case study of social theory teaching.
Author(s): Rosie, Anthony
Abstract: This paper draws on case-study data collected from undergraduate students taking courses in social theory. The paper sets out an approach to Sociology as a discipline that promotes an understanding of moral categories. Drawing the work of Bernstein, Benhabib and Hird, a model of 'generalised' and concrete other' provides a framework for understanding the discipline of Sociology and its pedagogy. A case study of student experience reveals the complexity of the 'concrete other' and how a more personalised and social interventionist account can be developed through Hird's concept of 'inner diversity'.

Title: Caroline Bartlett Crane and the history of sociology: Salvation...
Author(s): Rynbrandt, Linda J.
Abstract: Investigates the relationship between Progressive era (1890-1920) social reform and the origins of American sociology. Background information on social scientist Caroline Bartlett Crane; Perception of Bartlett on sociology.

Title: What Next?: Language and Social Interaction Study at the Century's Turn.
Author(s): Schegloff, Emanuel A.
Abstract: Provides information on a study which explored the macrosociological context and levels of interaction in the study of language and social interaction. Explanation on the essay `Politics As a Vocation,' by Max Weber; Views on the relation between language and talking in interaction; Attributes of social interaction.

Title: Durkheim, mortality and modernity: Collective effervescence, homo duplex and the sources of moral...
Author(s): Shilling, Chris; Mellor, Philip A.
Abstract: Focuses on how the revival of the interest in mortality will benefit from engaging creatively with the book `The Elementary Forms of Religious Life' by Durkheim. Relationship between collective effervescence, homo duplex and the social construction of moral orders; What is provided by the book; Details on homo duplex.

Practice Tests

Answers to these questions are found at the end of this manual.

Multiple Choice

_____ 1. The key feature of the sociological imagination is

    a. knowing the difference between sociology and the other social sciences.
    b. using sociological insights to make the world better.
    c. removing biases from one's study of other people.
    d. seeing the impact of social forces on our private lives.

_____ 2. _____ would first identify a social problem, gather data documenting the nature
    of the problem and then formulate a social-action policy based on the data.

    a. W.E.B. DuBois   c. Jane Addams
    b. Herbert Spencer   d. Herbert Blumer

_____ 3. Which of the following is NOT one of sociology's major perspectives?

    a. the structural functional   c. the neoclassical
    b. the conflict   d. the interactionist

_____ 4. Organic solidarity is usually a feature of

    a. complex rural societies.
    b. complex industrialized societies.
    c. simple, pastoral societies.
    d. postindustrial societies.

_____ 5. Max Weber argued that sociologists should use the research method of interpretive
    understanding, which is the use of

    a. statistical surveys.
    b. social work techniques.
    c. sympathetic understanding of subjects.
    d. active efforts to change society.

_____ 6. According to the conflict perspective, if women were treated more equally in the work force and received equal pay to that of men

    a. They would be unlikely to become prostitutes.
    b. They would be less likely to become housewives.
    c. They would be more likely to experience dominance over men.
    d. They would be more likely to become prostitutes.

_____ 7. Anne, a researcher studying human behavior in a college library, observed a young man sit down next to a young woman. Anne noted that when the young man smiled, the young woman frowned, stood up, and moved to another table. Which theoretical perspective was Anne using?

    a. functionalist _Institut_
    b. conflict

    c. interactionist
    d. structuralist

_____ 8. The research method most frequently used by sociologists is_____.

    a. the survey
    b. participant observation

    c. content analysis
    d. interviewing

_____ 9. In an experiment, six college students were placed in one room while six were placed in another. The first group of six was exposed to a certain treatment. This group is called the _____ group.

    a. observed
    b. sample

    c. control
    d. experimental

_____ 10. Postmodernist theory appears to be a hybrid of conflict and _____ perspectives.

    a. symbolic interaction
    b. functional

    c. convergence
    d. emergence

Fill In The Blank

organic solidarity

1. _____ is a type of social cohesion that arises when people perform a wide variety of specialized jobs.

out sourcing

2. The practice of producing inexpensive products by building factories and hiring workers abroad is called _____.

social marginality.

3. _____ is when certain members of a society are excluded from the mainstream.

Addams

4. In the United States, Jane _____ was the only sociologist ever to have received a Nobel prize.

small buses of ED—: Tax Eta Gove - vote

5. A tentative statement of how various events are related to one another is called a(an) _____. _Hypothesis._

True or False

_T_ 1. W.E.B. DuBois, an African American sociologist, founded the second department of sociology in the United States at Atlanta University.

_F_ 2. The micro view used by sociologists focuses on society at large.

_F_ 3. Organic solidarity is characteristic of simple _complex_ industrial societies.

_F_ 4. Patriarchy is a system of domination with women _men_ exercising power over men. _over woman-_

_T_ 5. Often times, sociologists do not identify themselves as researchers to the people they are studying.

Essay

1. Summarize the general contributions Europeans made to the development of modern sociology.

2. Discuss the focus of early American sociology.

3. Describe Durkheim's definitions of *mechanical* and *organic solidarity*.

4. State the main idea of *symbolic interactionism*. What is the role of symbols in this perspective?

5. Define *detached* and *participant observation*. What are the major differences between these two types of observation?

Chapter 1 Page 8 Class Conflict	Chapter 1 Page 11 Conflict Perspective
Chapter 1 Page 23 Content Analysis	Chapter 1 Page 23 Control Group
Chapter 1 Page 25 Deconstructionism	Chapter 1 Page 21 Detached Observation
Chapter 1 Page 4 Economic Globalization	Chapter 1 Page 22 Ethnography

A theoretical perspective that portrays society as always changing and always marked by conflict	Marx's term for the struggle between capitalists, who own the means of production, and the proletariat, who do not
The subjects in an experiment who are not exposed to the independent variable	Searching for specific words or ideas and then turning them into numbers
A method of observation in which the researcher observes as an outsider, from a distance, without getting involved	The idea that to understand society, we should deconstruct it, or take it apart, along with anything associated with it
An analysis of people's lives from their own perspectives	The interrelationship among the world's economies

Chapter 1 Page 22 Experiment	Chapter 1 Page 23 Experimental Group
Chapter 1 Page 12 Feminist Theory	Chapter 1 Page 10 Functionalist Perspective
Chapter 1 Page 4 Hypothesis	Chapter 1 Page 11 Latent Function
Chapter 1 Page 10 Macro View	Chapter 1 Page 22 Manifest Function

The group that is exposed to the independent variable	A research operation in which the researcher manipulates variables so that their influence can be determined
A theoretical perspective that focuses on social order	A form of conflict theory that explains human life in terms of the experiences of women
A function that is unintended and often unrecognized	A tentative statement about how various events are related to one another
A function that is intended and seems obvious	A view that focuses on the large social phenomena of society, such as social institutions and inequality

Chapter 1 Page 11 Mechanical Solidarity	Chapter 1 Page 10 Micro View
Chapter 1 Page 11 Organic Solidarity	Chapter 1 Page 4 Outsourcing
Chapter 1 Page 21 Participant Observation	Chapter 1 Page 13 Partiarchy
Chapter 1 Page 19 Population	Chapter 1 Page 20 Random Sample

A view that focuses on the immediate social situations in which people interact with one another	A form of social cohesion that develops when people do similar work and have similar beliefs and values
The practice of producing inexpensive products by building factories and hiring workers abroad	A type of social cohesion that arises when people in a society perform a wide variety of specialized jobs and therefore have to depend on one another
A system of domination in which men exercise power over women	A method of observing in which the researcher takes part in the activities of the group being studied
A sample drawn in such a way that all members of the population have an equal chance of being selected	The entire group of people to be studied

Chapter 1 Page 20 Sample	Chapter 1 Page 23 Secondary Analysis
Chapter 1 Page 11 Social Consensus	Chapter 1 Page 5 Social Forces
Chapter 1 Page 5 Social Integration	Chapter 1 Page 3 Social Marginality
Chapter 1 Page 5 Sociological Imagination	Chapter 1 Page 2 Sociology

Searching for new knowledge in the data collected earlier by another researcher or a public agency	A relatively small number of people selected from a larger population
Forces that arise from the society of which we are a part	A condition in which most members of society agree on what is good for everybody to have and cooperate to achieve it
Being excluded from mainstream society	The degree to which people are tied to a social group
The systematic, scientific study of human society	Mills' term for the ability to see the impact of social forces on individuals, especially in their private lives

Chapter 1 Page 20	Chapter 1 Page 20
Stratified Sampling	**Structured Interview**
Chapter 1 Page 19	Chapter 1 Page 23
Survey	**Symbolic Interactionist Perspective**
Chapter 1 Page 20	Chapter 1 Page 10
Systematic Sampling	**Theoretical Perspective**
Chapter 1 Page 5	Chapter 1 Page 21
Theory	**Unstructured Interview**

An interview in which the researcher asks standardized questions that require respondents to chose from among several standardized answers	The process of drawing a random sample in which various categories of people are represented in proportions equal to their presence in the population
A theoretical perspective that directs our attention to the details of a specific situation and of the interaction between individuals in that situation	A research method that involves asking questions about opinions, beliefs, or behaviors
A set of general assumptions about the nature of society	The process of drawing a random sample systematically rather than haphazardly
An interview in which open-ended questions are asked and the respondent is allowed to answer freely in his or her own words	A set of logically related hypotheses that explains the relationship among various phenomena

Chapter 1
Page 9

Verstehen

	Weber's term for empathetic understanding of the subjects studied by sociologists

Chapter 2: Sociology and Culture

Learning Objectives

After reading Chapter 2, the student should be able to:

1.   Define the key concept of society.
2.   Describe the basic building blocks of society, including status, role, groups and institutions.
3.   Define the concept of sociocultural evolution and the force the propels it.
4.   Analyze the evolution of five distinct types of large-scale social structures from small pre-industrial societies to the postindustrial society of today.
5.   Define the concept of culture, including both its ideational and material aspects, relate culture to the concept of society, and describe the several components of culture.
6.   Explore the basic values of U.S. culture, and discuss multiculturalism and pop culture.
7.   Undertake a global analysis of culture, including cultural universals, ethnocentrism, and cultural relativism.
8.   Examine the different sociological perspectives on culture.
9.   Explore the issues presented in the "Sociological Frontier" section on the new U.S. society emerging in the 21st century.
10. Analyze ways we can better interact with persons from different cultures as presented in the section on "Using Sociology."

Key Concepts

achieved status
Afrocentrism
agricultural society
ascribed status
belief
cultural integration
cultural relativism
cultural universals
culture
Eurocentrism
ethnocentrism
folkways
horticultural society
hunting-gathering society
industrial society
knowledge
laws
master status
material culture
mores

pastoral society
popular culture
postindustrial society
prescribed role
primary group
role
role conflict
role performance
role set
role strain
sanction
secondary group
social aggregate
social group
social institution
society
sociobiology
sociocultural evolution
status
status inconsistency

multiculturalism
nonmaterial culture
norms

subordinate status
symbol
value

Content Select Articles

The full text of the following articles can be found on the ContentSelect Sociology data base by searching for the article's author.

Title: Globalization and Trinidad Carnival: Diaspora, Hybridity, and Identity in Global Culture

Source: Cultural Studies, Oct99, Vol. 13 Issue 4, p661, 30p

Author(s):   Nurse, Keith

Abstract: Presents a case study of the impact and implications for global culture of periphery-to-center cultural flows in the context of the Trinidad carnival in Trinidad and Tobago. Impact of the carnival global and historical significance analysis on globalization theory; Basis for the carnival formation; Degree of core societies participation in globalization.

Title: Diversities of National Identity in a Multicultural Society: The Australian Case.

Source: National Identities, Jul2000, Vol. 2 Issue 2, p175, 12p

Author(s):   Jones, F. L.

Abstract: During the past half-century Australian immigration policy has moved from the assimilationist doctrine of Anglo-conformity, whereby non-British settlers were expected to adopt the Australian way-of-life, to a policy of multiculturalism that accepts and respects the cultures and traditions of newcomers, governed only by an overriding commitment to the basic institutions of Australian society. Newcomers are encouraged to take out Australian citizenship, which is available to immigrants after two years' residence, provided that they meet some other requirements, for example, the ability to speak and understand basic English. Notwithstanding changes in official policy, the population at large has a more diverse range of understandings of what it means to be 'truly Australian'. In this paper, I validate an earlier typology of such understandings and explore the social and attitudinal correlates of beliefs about Australian identity among four broad groupings of Australians: dogmatic nativists; literal nativists; civic nationalists; and moderate pluralists.

Title: Different habits, different hearts: The moral languages of the...

Source: American Sociologist, Spring98, Vol. 29 Issue 1, p83, 19p, 2 charts

Author(s):   Jensen, Lene Arnett

Abstract: Presents information on a study regarding moral languages of individualism and culture war on the society in the United States. Theoretical background on individualism and culture war; Methodology of the study; Discussions on the results.

Title: Spectacles of Ethnicity: Festivals and the Commodification of Ethnic Culture Among Louisiana...
Source: Sociological Spectrum, Oct-Dec2000, Vol. 20 Issue 4, p377, 31p, 4 charts
Author(s):   Bankston III, Carl L.

Abstract: Drawing on the example of the Louisiana Cajuns, an ethnic group that has been enjoying a wave of popular revival in recent years, this study suggests that changes in the perception of an ethnic identity are related to socioeconomic transformation. We identify the festival as a key aspect of the Cajun revival since the 1960s. An examination of the history, activities, and contemporary spatiotemporal organization of festivals reveals similarities to other aspects of a society of mass consumption. Niche marketing, the structuring of recreation around the modern work week, and the establishment of personal identity through the purchase of symbolically rich commodities are all embodied in present-day Cajun festivals. At the same time, the consumption of ethnic commodities is linked by the consumers with a sense of tradition and descent from a mythic past. The festivals of southwestern Louisiana are, in this sense, "invented traditions" and, paradoxically, a measure of the assimilation of this particular ethnic group into American culture.

Practice Tests

Answers to these questions are found at the end of this manual.

Multiple Choice

1. Research has shown that an individual's look has an impact on expectations of others as well as an impact on their earning power. The individual's looks would be called their _____ status by sociologists.

   a. master   c. self
   b. personality   d. influence

2. A college student who studies, spends time in the library, attends classes and submits assignments on time is following the _____ role for the status of student.

   a. assigned   c. prescribed
   b. social   d. scripted

3. Persons who are in the same space at the same time but who do not interact make up a (n)

   a. group.   c. aggregate.
   b. social network.   d. social category.

4. If a group's main source of food is domesticating and herding animals, what type of preindustrial society is it ?

   a. agricultural   c. hunting and gathering
   b. horticultural   d. pastoral

5. Which of the following is NOT a way the transition to a postindustrial society has begun to influence our lives?

   a. beliefs   c. genes
   b. objects   d. customs

6. Which of the following would NOT be considered a part of culture?

   a. the movement of people from large cities to small towns and rural areas
   b. the questioning of blind faith in science and technology
   c. the individual enjoying more power or freedom than ever before
   d. an increase in gender inequality

7. Which are relatively "weak" norms, expecting us to behave properly in everyday life?

   a. mores   c. laws
   b. folkways   d. sanction

8. Americans have a large number of words that refer to automobiles. For sociologists, this fact suggests that Americans

   a. own too many automobiles.
   b. really do not like automobiles.
   c. consider automobiles important.
   d. have extensive vocabularies.

9. Many Americans vote against taxes to support persons on welfare. What traditional American cultural value might have guided this pattern of voting?

   a. dislike of the poor   c. kindness
   b. self-reliance   d. freedom

10. Which of the following is an example of popular culture?

   a. a symphony   c. opera
   b. symbols   d. rap music

Fill In The Blank

1. The belief that a culture must be understood on its own terms is known as _Culture_. *Relativism* ~~Mead~~

2. _Pop_ culture is a collection of relatively unsophisticated artistic creations that appeal to a mass audience.

3. The array of roles attached to one particular status is called a(n) _Role_ . *Set*

4. A society that depends on growing plans in small gardens for its survival in called a _Horticulture_ society.

5. The view of the world from the standpoint of African culture is called _Afrocentrism_

True or False

_T_ 1. Every status has rights and responsibilities.

_F_ 2. The industrial revolution started in Italy over 200 years ago.

_T_ 3. Stealing a car is considered to be a violation of social mores.

_F_ 4. Appreciation of multiculturalism has not increased in the United States over the past fifty years.

_F_ 5. Sociological studies suggest that cultural values such as human rights and equality, are important to all societies.

Essay

1. Define *society* and identify the key building blocks of society.

2. Define the *basic components* of society, including *status, role, groups, and institutions.*

3. Discuss how *horticulturalists* differ from *pastoralists* and *hunter-gathers.*

4. Define *culture,* identifying how material and non-material culture relate to the overall concept of culture.

5. Describe how *ethnocentrism* leads to bias against other cultures.

Chapter 2 Page 33 Achieved Status	Chapter 2 Page 50 Afrocentrism
Chapter 2 Page 39 Agricultural Society	Chapter 2 Page 32 Ascribed Status
Chapter 2 Page 43 Belief	Chapter 2 Page 48 Cultural Integration
Chapter 2 Page 56 Cultural Relativism	Chapter 2 Page 53 Cultural Universals

The view of the world from the standpoint of African culture	The status that is attained through an individual's own actions
The status that one has no control over, such as status based on race, gender, or age	A society that produces food primarily by using plows and draft animals on the farm
The joining of various values into a coherent whole	An idea that is relatively subjective, unreliable, or unverifiable
Practices found in all cultures as the means for meeting the same human needs	The belief that a culture must be understood on its own terms

Chapter 2 Page 42 Culture	Chapter 2 Page 56 Ethnocentrism
Chapter 2 Page 50 Eurocentrism	Chapter 2 Page 44 Folkways
Chapter 2 Page 39 Horticultural Society	Chapter 2 Page 37 Hunting-Gathering Society
Chapter 2 Page 40 Industrial Society	Chapter 2 Page 43 Knowledge

The attitude that one's own culture is superior to those of other people's	A design for living or a complex whole consisting of objects, values, and other characteristics that people acquire as members of society
Weak norms that specify expectations about proper behavior	A view of the world from the standpoint of European culture
A society that hunts animals and gathers plants as its primary means for survival	A society that produces food primarily by growing plants in small gardens
A collection of relatively objective ideas and facts about the physical and social worlds	A society that produces food for its subsistence primarily by using machinery

Chapter 2 Page 45 Laws	Chapter 2 Page 33 Master Status
Chapter 2 Page 42 Material Culture	Chapter 2 Page 44 Mores
Chapter 2 Page 48 Multiculturalism	Chapter 2 Page 42 Nonmaterial Culture
Chapter 2 Page 43 Norm	Chapter 2 Page 38 Pastoral Society

A status that dominates a relationship	Norms that are specified formally in writing and backed by the power of the state
Strong norms that specify normal behavior and constitute demands, not just expectations	Every conceivable kind of physical object produced by humans
The intangible aspect of culture	A state in which all subcultures in the same society are equal to one another
A society that domesticates and herds animals as its primary source of food	A social rule that specifies how people should behave

Chapter 2 Page 50 ## Popular Culture	Chapter 2 Page 41 ## Postindustrial Society
Chapter 2 Page 34 ## Prescribed Role	Chapter 2 Page 34 ## Primary Group
Chapter 2 Page 34 ## Role	Chapter 2 Page 34 ## Role Conflict
Chapter 2 Page 34 ## Role Performance	Chapter 2 Page 34 ## Role Set

A society that produces food so efficiently that high technology and service dominate it	A collection of relatively unsophisticated artistic creations that appeal to a mass audience
A group whose members interact informally, relate to each other as whole persons, and enjoy their relationship for its own sake	The expectation held by society regarding how an individual with a particular status should behave
Conflict between the roles of two different status being played simultaneously	A set of expectations of what individuals should do in accordance with a particular status that they hold
An array of roles attached to one particular status	Actual performance of a role

Chapter 2 Page 34 Role Strain	Chapter 2 Page 45 Sanction
Chapter 2 Page 35 Secondary Group	Chapter 2 Page 35 Social Aggregate
Chapter 2 Page 35 Social Group	Chapter 2 Page 35 Social Institution
Chapter 2 Page 32 Society	Chapter 2 Page 53 Sociobiology

A reward for conforming to norms or punishment for violation of norms	Stress caused by incompatible demands from the role of a single status
A number of people who happen to be in one place but do not interact with one another	A group whose members interact formally, relate to each other as players of particular roles, and expect to profit from each other
A set of widely shared beliefs, norms, and procedures necessary for meeting the basic needs of a society	A collection of people who interact with one another and have a certain feeling of unity
A new Darwinian theory that human behavior is genetically determined	A collection of interacting individuals sharing the same way of life and living in the same territory

Chapter 2 Page 36 Sociocultural Evolution	Chapter 2 Page 32 Status
Chapter 2 Page 33 Status Inconsistency	Chapter 2 Page 33 Subordinate Status
Chapter 2 Page 46 Symbol	Chapter 2 Page 43 Value

A position in a group or society	The process of changing from a technologically simple society to a more complex one, with significant consequences for social and cultural life
A status that does not dominate a relationship; the opposite of master status	A condition in which the same individual is given two conflicting status rankings
A socially shared idea about what is good, desirable, or important	A word, gesture, music, or anything that stands for some other thing

Chapter 3: Socialization

Learning Objectives

After reading Chapter 3, the student should be able to:

1.   Define the key concepts of socialization and personality.
2.   Analyze the significance of heredity in determining intelligence and aptitude.
3.   Analyze the role of the environment in shaping personality, and discuss the experiences of isolated children and geniuses.
4.   Describe the process of socialization in terms of several theories of personality development, including Freud's theory of psychosexual development, Piaget's theory of cognitive development, and feminist theory.
5.   Examine the three sociological perspectives on socialization.
6.   Explore socialization in some of America's socially diverse subcultures.
7.   Examine socialization from a global perspective.
8.   Describe and illustrate the different agents of socialization, including the family, school, and mass media.
9.   Outline the types of adult socialization, Erikson's theory of the adult life cycle, and Elizabeth Kübler-Ross' analysis of dying.
10.   Answer the question, "Are We Puppets of Society?"
11.   Explore the sociological frontier of peer parenting, with emphasis on a crisis of authority among parents of teenage children.
12.   Analyze how to use sociology to make latchkey kids safe and smart.

Key Concepts

anticipatory socialization
aptitude
conventional morality
developmental socialization
ego
gender identity
generalized other
id
intelligence

looking-glass self
peer group
personality
postconventional morality
preconventional morality
resocialization
significant others
socialization
superego
total institutions

Content Select Articles

[Note: The following articles are available to students through ContentSlect, a data base of sociological articles that students can use through purchase of the text. They can be found in the data base by typing in the author's name.]

Title: Intergenerational Influences on the Entry into Parenthood: Mothers'
            Preferences for Family and Nonfamily Behavior.
Source: Social Forces, Sep2000, Vol. 79 Issue 1, p319, 30p
Author(s): Barber, Jennifer S.
Abstract: This article examines the extent to which childbearing behavior is
            determined by mothers' preferences versus individuals' own preferences.
            The theoretical framework is based on *socialization* and social control. A
            total of 835 mother-child pairs from the Intergenerational Panel Study of
            Parents and Children, a long-term longitudinal study, are analyzed using
            hazard models. The empirical analyses show that both sons and
            daughters whose mothers prefer early marriage, large families, low levels
            of education, and stay-at-home mothers enter parenthood earlier than
            their peers, and analyses show support for both *socialization* and social
            control mechanisms.

Title: Sexual Messages on Television: Comparing Findings From Three Studies.
Source: Journal of Sex Research, Aug99, Vol. 36 Issue 3, p230, 7p, 4 charts,
            2 graphs
Author(s): Kunkel, Dale; Cope, Kirstie M.
Abstract: Television portrayals may contribute to the sexual *socialization* of children
            and adolescents, and therefore it is important to examine the patterns of
            sexual content presented on television. This report presents a summary
            view across three related studies of sexual messages on television. The
            content examined ranges from programs most popular with adolescents
            to a comprehensive, composite week sample of shows aired across the
            full range of broadcast and cable channels. The results across the three
            studies identify a number of consistent patterns in television's treatment
            of sexual content.

Title: Preadolescents and Apparel Purchasing: Conformity to Parents and Peers
            in the Consumer *Socialization* Process.
Source: Journal of Social Behavior & Personality, Jun2000, Vol. 15 Issue 2,
            p243, 15p,
Author(s): Meyer, Deborah J.C.; Anderson, Heather C.
Abstract: Preadolescents are spending more money on consumer goods than any
            other time in history. Although the interest in the adolescent (children
            aged 13-18) market has stimulated much research, little attention has
            focused on the years of preadolescence, ages 8-12. During this period
            children begin making product decisions and building a foundation of
            product knowledge. Information about the preadolescent child and the
            important role that conformity to parents and peers plays in apparel
            purchasing is necessary for researchers and educators to understand how
            these consumers are socialized. The purpose of this research is to examine
            the extent to which conformity motivators influence shopping behavior

Title: The Roots of Evil: Social Conditions, Culture, Personality, and Basic Human Needs.
Source: Personality & Social Psychology Review, 1999, Vol. 3 Issue 3, p179, 14p
Author(s): Staub, Ervin

Abstract: Focuses on the origins of evil in several domains. Account on the instigating conditions leading to collective violence; Examination on the *socialization* and experience of youth leading to aggression; Relevance of personal characteristics and a system of relationships to sexual abuse.

Practice Tests

Answers to these questions are found at the end of this manual.

Multiple Choice

1. As Judy grew up, she developed a distinctive personality that set her apart from other women. Sociologists would explain that these differences probably resulted from

   a. biological factors.
   b. abnormal personality development.
   c. a unique pattern of socialization.
   d. a product of chance.

2. Intelligence is

   a. inherited.
   b. the capacity and temperament that determines whether we will succeed in life.
   c. the capacity for developing physical or social skills.
   d. the capacity for mental achievement.

3. Piaget's work focused on the ___Cognitive___ part of human personality.

   a. cognitive   c. behavioral
   b. motivational   d. moral

4. George Herbert Mead referred to the process of putting ourselves in the place of others as *Role Taking*

   a. role playing.
   b. perceiving the generalized others.
   c. role-taking.
   d. the looking-glass self.

_A_ 5. Research has suggested that middle-class families, when compared to lower-class
families, are

    a. more authoritarian.
    b. more permissive.
    c. less sensitive to the child's feelings.
    d. less strict.

_C_ 6. The task of socializing a society's members is the responsibility of several groups and
institutions. Sociologists call these entities

    a. socializers.   c. socializing agents.
    b. teachers.   d. socializing parents.

_D_ 7. A group whose members is about the same age and has the same interest is called a(n)
_____ group.

    a. secondary   c. primary
    b. non   d. peer

_A_ 8. Which of the following is an outcome of poor economic conditions on parenting?

    a. parental nurturance declines
    b. stronger family ties and nurturing develop
    c. little changes, because parenting is an individual matter
    d. parental discipline increases

_C_ 9. In a total institution, inmates are dehumanized. Goffman called this process

    a. socialization.   c. mortification of the self.
    b. identity bargaining.   d. losing sight of original goals.

_D_ 10. According to the author of the text, the permissive socialization of Western children
may be changing to

    a. conformity.   c. non-conformity.
    b. over-permissiveness   d. non-permissiveness

Fill In The Blank

1. _Conventional_ morality was Kohlberg's term for the practice of defining right and wrong according to the motive being judged.

2. _Developmental_ socialization is the process by which people learn to be more competent in playing their currently assumed roles.

3. _Resocialization_ is the process by which people are forced to abandon their old self and to develop a new self in its place.

4. At home, children are treated as special persons. At school they are are treated more _Impersonal_

5. The _Peer_ group teaches it members to be independent of adult authorities.

True or False

_T_ 1. Intelligence is both inherited and learned.

_F_ 2. Well-fed infants will be come physically and psychologically developed.

_T_ 3. George Herbert Mean was one of the founders of the symbolic interactionist perspective.

_F_ 4. The family is the least important agent of socialization.

_T_ 5. Western parents are more likely to treat their children as adults than non-western parents.

Essay

1. Define the key concepts of *socialization*. What is the impact of *nature* and *nurture* on the socialization process?

2. Define *gender identities*. What is the role of family, school, and the mass media in *gender development*?

3. Discuss Erickson's three stages of the adult life cycle. How have feminists criticized Erickson's theory?

4. Describe how the status of the *elderly* differs in traditional and modern societies.

5. Describe ways in which we sometimes act like *puppets of society*. When do we do things differently than dictated by society?

Chapter 3 Page 84 Anticipatory Socialization	Chapter 3 Page 60 Aptitude
Chapter 3 Page 72 Conventional Morality	Chapter 3 Page 84 Developmental Socialization
Chapter 3 Page 71 Ego	Chapter 3 Page 73 Gender Identity
Chapter 3 Page 76 Generalized Others	Chapter 3 Page 71 Id

The capacity for developing physical or social skills	The process by which an individual learns to assume a role for the future
The process by which people learn to be more competent in playing their currently assumed roles	Kohlberg's term for the practice of defining right and wrong according to the *motive* of the action being judged
People's images of what they are socially expected to be and do on the basis of their sex	Freud's term for the part of personality that is rational, dealing with the world logically and realistically
Freud's term for the part of personality that is irrational, concerned only with seeking pleasure	Mead's term for people who do not have close ties to a child but who do influence a child's internalization of society's values

Chapter 3 Page 66 Intelligence	Chapter 3 Page 75 Looking-Glass Self
Chapter 3 Page 82 Peer Group	Chapter 3 Page 66 Personality
Chapter 3 Page 73 Postconventional Morality	Chapter 3 Page 72 Preconventional Morality
Chapter 3 Page 84 Resocialization	Chapter 3 Page 75 Significant Others

Cooley's term for the self-image that we develop from the way others treat us	The capacity for mental or intellectual achievement
A fairly stable configuration of feelings attitudes, ideas, and behaviors that characterizes an individual	A group whose members are about the same age and have similar interests
Kohlberg's term for the practice of defining right and wrong according to the *consequences* of the action being judged	Kohlberg's term for the practice of judging actions by taking into account the importance of *conflicting norms*
Mead's term for people who have close ties to a child and exert a strong influence on the child	The process by which people are forced to abandon their old selves and develop new ones

Chapter 3 Page 66 Socialization	Chapter 3 Page 71 Superego
Chapter 3 Page 84 Total Institutions	

Freud's term for the part of personality that is moral; popularly known as *conscience*	The process by which a society transmits its cultural values to its members
	Places where people are not only cut off from the larger society but also rigidly controlled by the administrators

Chapter 4: Social Interaction in Everyday Life

Learning Objectives

After reading Chapter 4, the student should be able to:

1. Define social interaction, compare oppositional, supportive, and symbolic interactions, and outline the three sociological perspectives on social interaction
2. Describe interaction as symbolic communication.
3. Examine the communication between women and men, or genderlects.
4. Define dramaturgy, and describe its different forms.
5. Describe the art and techniques of managing impressions.
6. Discuss the social construction of reality, including the Thomas Theorem, thnomethodology, and humorology.
7. Explore the sociological frontier of the world of online chat.
8. Understand how to use humor to improve your life.

Key Concepts

competition
conflict
cooperation
dramaturgy
ethnomethodology
exchange
genderlects
humorology
interaction ritual

kinesics
oppositional interaction
proxemics
role distance
social construction of reality
social interaction
supportive interaction
symbolic interaction
Thomas theorem

Content Select Articles

[Note: The following articles are available to students through ContentSelect, a data base of sociological articles that students can use through purchase of the text. They can be found in the data base by typing in the author's name.]

Title:	Conversation Analysis: A quest for order in *social interaction* and language use.
Source:	Acta Sociologica, 1999, Vol. 42 Issue 3, p251, 7p
Author(s):	Arminen, Ilkka
Abstract:	Focuses on the role of conversation analysis (CA) in *social interaction* and language use. Data collection method of CA; Basic idea of CA; Origins and development of CA; Comparison between CA and other *social*

scientific schools of thoughts; Relationship between linguistics and CA; Application of CA in the study of human-computer *interactions*

Title: Staging *Social* Structures: Ritual and *Social* Organisation in an Egalitarian Society. The Pastoral Pokot of Northern Kenya.

Source: Ethnos: Journal of Anthropology, Nov2000, Vol. 65 Issue 3, p341, 25p

Author(s): Bollig, Michael

Abstract: Investigates the agency aspect of pastoral Pokot in northern Kenya. *Social* exchange in the institutions of descent and age grading; Analysis on the case of pastoral Pokot in a historical context; Observation on the adoption of mobile livestock husbandry, exchange networks and *social interaction* of a group.

Title: Classroom "Families": Cooperating or Competing-Girls' and Boys' Interactional Styles in a Bilingual Classroom.

Source: Research on Language & Social Interaction, Jan2001, Vol. 34 Issue 1, p107, 24p

Author(s): Cook-Gumperz, Jenny; Szymanski, Margaret

Abstract: This article examines how students use gendered discourse practices in small peer group settings to accomplish their school tasks. The analysis contributes to the separate worlds hypothesis by showing how Latino children interactionally orient to their peer group as a gendered context. For 1 academic year, observations were made in an elementary bilingual classroom. The target 3rd-grade teacher referred to her student groups as "families," a label that emerged as a legitimizing metaphor for the group's collective action. In cooperating and competing to accomplish their school tasks, the students strategically used Spanish and English.

Title: Pillow Talk?

Source: Research on Language & Social Interaction, 1999, Vol. 32 Issue 1/2, p41, 10p

Author(s): Fitch, Kristine L.

Abstract: Explores pieces of *interaction* sequence enacted on an academic hotline for the study of *social interaction* and language. What constitutes a speech community; Resources people bring to bear on *interaction*; What culturally situated patterns and interactional/symbolic forms of personal relationship have an impact on culture

Practice Tests

Answers to these questions are found at the end of this manual.

Multiple Choice

A 1. The process by which individuals act toward and react to others is called

    a. social interaction.
    b. social structure.
    c. a social function.
    d. role playing.

D 2. Two types of supportive interactions are _____ and cooperation.

    a. conflict   c. competition
    b. prayer   d. exchange

D 3. If people do not show respect for each other through social interaction, they will

    a. switch from oppositional interaction to supportive interaction.
    b. try harder to establish social interaction.
    c. create new forms of language to show respect.
    d. more likely upset the social order.

C 4. The use of body movements as a means of communication is called

    a. fixed communication.   c. kinesics.
    b. supportive communication.   d. proxemics.

B 5. Women have a private speaking style that emphasizes the showing of feelings. Their style is an example of

    a. genderlect.   c. report-talk.
    b. rapport-talk   d. emotion-talk.

Role Distance 6. _____ is the separation of our role playing as outward performance from our inner self.

    a. role playing   c. role distance
    b. social interaction   d. social status

_____ 7. Goffman's analysis of performances points out that audiences work together with the performer to create an impression. Which of the following is NOT one of these ways of support?

    a. dramaturgical acting   c. dramaturgical loyalty
    b. dramaturgical discipline   d. dramaturgical circumspection

_____ 8. John was an actor. A part of his performance involved misrepresenting a person's motives, but he did so with humor in his voice. This is an example of how performers

    a. dupe audiences.
    b. make audience assistance possible.
    c. make fools of themselves.
    d. create humor.

_____ 9. The Thomas Theorem is sometimes called the

    a. self-fulfilling prophecy.
    b. face-saving prophesy.
    c. humorology perspective.
    d. construction of reality perspective.

_____ 10. Sociologist Murray David concludes that _Humor_ is an attack on culture and society.

    a. socialization   c. language
    b. dramaturgy   d. humor

Fill In The Blank

1.1 _Exchange_ is when two people offer each other something in order to get something in return.

2. The process by which individuals act toward and react to others is called _Social_ interaction.

3. The study of the amount of space a person takes around himself or herself is called _Proxemics_

4. Being polite, courteous, or nice, which shows reverence to the other, are examples of interaction _Rituals_.

5. Separating the role-playing as outward performance from the inner self is called role _Distance_

True or False

__T__ 1. Competition hampers achievement because it is stressful.

__F__ 2. The Viet Nam War was a unifying force for the American society.

__F__ 3. Men are more prone than women to express their feelings.

__F__ 4. Sociologically, on line chat is the same as face-to-face interaction.

__T__ 5. A Canadian study has shown that stressed people who laugh at funny stories become less depressed.

Essay

1. Define an *exchange*. How does the *norm of reciprocity* operate within an exchange?

2. Identify how *body language* varies from one culture to another.

3. In what ways are *interaction rituals* like religious rituals?

4. Summarize the reasons why audiences are motivated to be tactful.

5. Define *humor* and explain why an incongruity between two realities can create humor.

Chapter 4 Page 95 Competition	Chapter 4 Page 95 Conflict
Chapter 4 Page 94 Cooperation	Chapter 4 Page 104 Dramaturgy
Chapter 4 Page 108 Ethnomethodology	Chapter 4 Page 94 Exchange
Chapter 4 Page 94 Genderlects	Chapter 4 Page 109 Humorology

An interaction in which two individuals disregard any rules, each trying to achieve his or her own goal by defeating each other	An interaction in which two individuals must follow mutually accepted rules, each trying to achieve the same goal before the other does
A method of analyzing social interactions as if the participants were performing on a stage	An interaction in which two or more individuals work together to achieve a common goal
An interaction in which two individuals offer each other something in order to obtain a reward in return	The analysis of how people define the world in which they live
The study or practice of humor	**Linguistic styles that reflect the different worlds of women and men**

Chapter 4 Page 106 # Interaction Ritual	Chapter 4 Page 99 # Kinesics
Chapter 4 Page 94 # Oppositional Interaction	Chapter 4 Page 99 # Proxemics
Chapter 4 Page 105 # Role Distance	Chapter 4 Page 108 # Social Construction of Reality
Chapter 4 Page 94 # Social Interaction	Chapter 4 Page 94 # Supportive Interaction

The use of body movements as a means of communication; also called *body language*	A form of interaction in which the participants perform certain acts to show reverence to each other
The use of space as a means of communication	An interaction in which the participants treat each other as competitors or enemies
The process by which people create through social interaction a certain idea, feeling, or belief about the enviromnent	Separating role-playing as outward performance from the inner self
An interaction in which the participants treat each other as supporters or friends	The process by which individuals act toward and react to others

Chapter 4
Page 94

Symbolic Interaction

Chapter 4
Page 108

Thomas Theorem

Sociologist W.I. Thomas' famous pronouncement that "if people define situations as real, they are real in their consequences"	An interaction in which people actively interpret each other's actions and reactions and behave in accordance with the interpretation

Chapter 5: Groups and Organizations

Learning Objectives

After reading Chapter 5, the student should be able to:

1.   Understand how much of our lives is influenced by groups.
2.   Define a social group and show how it differs from social aggregates and categories.
3.   Describe the several types of groups important to sociology, such as primary and secondary groups, reference groups and ingroups/outgroups.
4.   Analyze several characteristics of groups such as the impact of group size and group leadership, and the impact of diversity on groups.
5.   Describe the attributes and effects of social networks.
6.   Outline the characteristics of formal organizations, and list the means organizations use, such as rational planning and division of labor, to achieve their goals.
7.   Describe the functionalist perspective on organizations, and the scientific management and human relations models it supports.
8.   Study the conflict perspective on organizations and the collectivist and feminist models.
9.   Examine the symbolic interactionist perspective on organizations, including organizational culture and bureaucracy.
10. Recount some of the realities of bureaucracy, including bureaucratic benefits, problems and future prospects.
11. Describe a global view of groups and organizations.
12. Research social isolation on the net, as presented in the Sociological Frontiers box.
13. Analyze reducing wait time on lines as explained in the Using Sociology box.

Key Concepts

bureaucracy
expressive leaders
formal organization
"groupthink"
idiosyncrasy credit
informal organization
in-group
instrumental leaders
Laissez-faire leaders

normative theories
out-group
Parkinson's Law
Peter Principle
rationalization
reference group
social aggregate
social category
social group
social network

Content Select Articles

[Note: The following articles are available to students through ContentSelect, a data base of sociological articles that students can use through purchase of the text. They can be found in the data base by typing in the author's name.]

Title:	Infrastructure and Institutional Change in the Networked University.
Source:	Information Communication & Society, Dec2000, Vol. 3 Issue 4, p494, 14p
Author(s):	Agre, Philip E.
Abstract:	Many people believe that information technology will bring massive structural changes to the university. This paper draws on concepts from both computer science and social theory to explore what these structural changes might be like. The point of departure is the observation that the interaction between information technology and market economics creates incentives to standardize the world. Standardization can be a force for good or evil, depending on how it is done, and this paper develops normative ideas about the relation between the forces of standardization and the places in which university teaching is done. Information technology allows these places to be more diverse than in the past, and a good rule of thumb is that the places in which learning occurs should be analogous in their structure and workings to the places in which the learned knowledge will be used. Universities can support this increased diversity of learning places with appropriate structural reforms, including decentralized governance and explicit attention to certain aspects of the university organization, such as media services and the career centre, that, historically, have been marginalized.

Title:	Informal Ties of the Unmarried in Middle and Later Life: Who Has Them and Who Does Not?
Source:	Sociological Spectrum, Apr-Jun2000, Vol. 20 Issue 2, p221, 18p, 2 charts
Author(s):	Keith, Pat M.; Kim, Soyoung; Schafer, Robert B.
Abstract:	Gender, marital status, age, and race were considered in relation to the amount and assessment of social ties among 1,124 unmarried men and women aged 40 and over. When there were significant effects of marital status, widowed people tended to be advantaged in amount and supportiveness of their informal ties, although the influence of marital status was affected by age and race. Contrary to some literature, gender differences in social relationships favoring women were not consistently observed. The oldest never married may have the greatest potential needs for affective and instrumental support.

Title:	The Net as a foraging society: Flexible communities.
Source:	Information Society, Apr-Jun98, Vol. 14 Issue 2, p97, 10p
Author(s):	Komito, Lee
Abstract:	Examines nonindustrial foraging societies in order to reveal the wide varieties and definitions of community that can exist. Various social groups which the term society can refer to; Examination of the Internet as a foraging society; Characteristics exhibited by social groups in foraging societies.

Title: Solomon Asch's Legacy for Group Research.
Source: Personality & Social Psychology Review, 1999, Vol. 3 Issue 4, p358, 7p
Author(s): Levine, John M.
Abstract: Asch's work has had a profound impact on how psychologists think about and study social influence in groups. To appreciate this impact, we must go beyond his classic conformity experiments and consider his broader theoretical framework. This article examines 4 of Asch's ideas that have proven to be particularly influential in later efforts to understand social influence in groups: (a) Social interaction depends on individuals' ability to represent others' positions, define themselves as members of the same group, and regulate their behavior in terms of the norms and values of the group; (b) independence is critical to effective group functioning; (c) independence and conformity are not simply mirror images that can be explained in terms of a unitary psychological process; and (d) change of meaning is an important mechanism of social influence. Finally, Asch's role as a theorist and researcher in the wider area of group dynamics is considered.]

Title: Making people work: Control and incentives in Swedish organizations.
Source: Acta Sociologica, 1999, Vol. 42 Issue 2, p103, 20p, 5 charts
Author(s): Szulkin, Ryszard
Abstract: Examines the correralation between control and incentive systems in different work structures. Concepts on alienation and corporalist theories of organization; Implementation of control; Mechanics on the distribution of incentives; Issues on bureaucracy; Discussion on decision-making power in organizations.

Practice Tests

Answers to these questions are found at the end of this manual.

Multiple Choice

1. A group of women is standing on the street corner waiting for the light to change so they can cross. Sociologists would call this collection of people a (n) social

   a. aggregate   c. group
   b. category   d. collection

2. The type of group that influences our behavior, but to which we do not necessarily belong, is called a

   a. formal organization.   c. secondary group.
   b. primary group.   d. reference group.

D 3. Which of the following groups is most likely to be a primary group?

    a. a labor union   c. students in Sociology 1310
    b. a political party   d. members of a fraternity

B 4. The Asch experiment, in which a group of subjects was asked to compare length of lines, demonstrates that groups

    a. allow people to feel free to express independent thought.
    b. have power to bring about conformity of its members.
    c. pressure members to agree with the leader of the group.
    d. have power to bring about compliance for the minority group members.

D 5. Which of the following is NOT one of the types of group leaders discussed in the text.

    a. instrumental   c. laissez-faire
    b. expressive   d. bureaucratic

D 6. All of the following are means organizations use to accomplish their goals, EXCEPT for

    a. rational planning.   c. a hierarchy of control.
    b. a division of labor.   d. a frame of reference.

B 7. The author of the text classifies several theories of organizational behavior based on how they

    a. view the problems of the individual worker or members.
    b. may have been influenced by the three major sociological perspectives.
    c. reflect different models of human behavior.
    d. create profits for their owners.

B 8. One criticism of the scientific management model is that it

    a. only emphasizes the official organization.
    b. treats workers as machines.
    c. contributes to worker dissatisfaction.
    d. contributes to the informal organization of workers.

C 9. The feminist model of organizations does more than get everybody to work together as equals. It also calls for

    a. tough collective bargaining.
    b. a strong formal structure.
    c. participation of all members.
    d. personal and emotional support from each other.

_D_ 10. According to the author, bureaucracy will probably _____ in the future.

    a. decline   c. overwhelm collective organization
    b. disappear   d. continue to thrive

Fill In The Blank

1. Leaders who achieve their group's goal by getting others to focus on task performance are _Instrumental_ leaders.

2. Cyberspace provides the opportunity for people all over the world to be involved in a computer _network_.

3. Unlike the bureaucratic model, the _Collectivist_ model foresees minimal division of labor and greater egalitarianism.

4. _Scientific_ management theory assumes that the primary goal of an organization is to maximize efficiency.

5. Companies such as Honda and General Motors sought to increase worker morale and productivity by introducing _quality_ circles.

True or False

_T_ 1. In preindustrial societies, most social life took place in primary groups.

_F_ 2. Experimental studies have found that group members tend NOT to submit to group conformity.

_F_ 3. A formal organization is not designed to pursue certain values and goals.

_T_ 4. Mayo argued that workers will reject management's offer of higher wages for higher production if co-workers are against working too hard.

_F_ 5. According to the conflict perspective, the practice of equality in an organization does not assure organizational success.

Essay

1. Define *reference group* and explain why they have a powerful influence on our behavior and attitudes.

2. Define *social network* and describe a small social network to which you belong.

3. Who developed the *scientific management* model. What were the major ideas of this theory?

4. From where did the *feminist organization* model originate? What are the distinctive features of this model?

5. Describe the differences between *bureaucracy in theory* and *bureaucracy in reality*. Why do these differences occur?

Chapter 5 Page 131 Bureaucracy	Chapter 5 Page 119 Expressive Leaders
Chapter 5 Page 125 Formal Organization	Chapter 5 Page 121 Groupthink
Chapter 5 Page 119 Idiosyncrasy Credit	Chapter 5 Page 128 Informal Organization
Chapter 5 Page 116 In-Group	Chapter 5 Page 119 Instrumental Leaders

Leaders who achieve group harmony by making others feel good	A modern Western organization defined by Max Weber as being rational in achieving its goals efficiently
The tendency for members of a cohesive group to maintain consensus to the extent of ignoring the truth	A group whose activities are rationally designed to achieve specific goals
A group formed by the informal relationships among members of an organization – based on personal interaction, not on any plan by the organization	The privilege that allows leaders to deviate from their group's norms
Leaders who achieve their group's goal by getting others to focus on task performance	The group to which an individual is strongly tied as a member

Chapter 5
Page 119

Laissez-Faire Leaders

Chapter 5
Page 133

Normative Theories

Chapter 5
Page 116

Out-Group

Chapter 5
Page 134

Parkinson's Law

Chapter 5
Page 134

Peter Principle

Chapter 5
Page 131

Rationalization

Chapter 5
Page 117

Reference Group

Chapter 5
Page 116

Social Aggregate

Theories that suggest what we should do to achieve our goals	Leaders who let others do their work more or less on their own
The observation that "Work expands to fill the time available for its completion"	A group of which an individual is not a member
Max Weber's term for the process of replacing subjective, spontaneous, informal, and diverse ways of doing things with a planned, objective, formally unified method based on abstract rules	The observation that "In every hierarchy, every employee tends to rise to his or her level of incompetence"
A number of people who happen to be in one place but do not interact with one another	A group that is used as a frame of reference for evaluating one's own behavior

Chapter 5 Page 116 Social Category	Chapter 5 Page 116 Social Group
Chapter 5 Page 123 Social Network	

A collection of people who interact with one another and have certain feelings of unity	A number of people who have something in common but who neither interact with one another not gather in one place
	A web of social relationships that link individuals or groups to one another

Chapter 6: Deviance and Control

Learning Objectives

After reading Chapter 6, the student should be able to:

1. State why deviance is so widespread and why our thinking about it is often erroneous.
2. Define deviance.
3. Analyze several examples of deviance, including homicide and rape, and outline their impact on American society.
4. Explain the functionalist perspective on deviance, and outline functionalist, strain, control and shaming theories.
5. Outline the conflict perspective on deviance, and explain conflict, power, and feminist theory.
6. State the symbolic interactionist perspective on deviance, and outline the differential association, labeling and phenomenological theories.
7. Analyze the impact of social diversity on deviance.
8. Examine deviance from a global perspective.
9. Outline our society's way of controlling deviance, with emphasis on the war on drugs.
10. Analyze the Sociological Frontier of shyness as a form of disease.
11. Review the "Putting it into Practice" box on how to manage one's drinking.

Key Concepts

anomie
deviance
differential association
disintegrative shaming
marginal surplus population
medicalization of deviance
neurosis

pornography
primary deviance
psychosis
rape
reintegrative shaming
relative deprivation
secondary deviance

Content Select Articles

[Note: The following articles are available to students through ContentSelect, a data base of sociological articles that students can use through purchase of the text. They can be found in the data base by typing in the author's name.]

Title: Is Deviance 'Dead'? The Decline of a Sociological Research Specialization.
Source: American Sociologist, Fall2001, Vol. 32 Issue 3, p43, 17p, 4 charts
Author(s): Miller, J. Mitchell; Wright, Richard A.
Abstract: Colin Sumner has declared that the sociology of deviance as a research specialty was 'dead' by 1975; later influential studies on norm-violating behavior appeared only in the specific area of criminology. We subjected this argument to empirical test through an analysis of the most-cited scholars and works in 263 textbooks, articles, and research notes umner's claims: The majority of the most-cited scholars in deviance today conduct research, primarily in criminology.

Title: Relation of General Deviance to Academic Dishonesty.
Source: Ethics & Behavior, Jan2000, Vol. 10 Issue 1, p1, 12p, 3 charts
Author(s): Blankenship, Kevin L.; Whitley Jr., Bernard E.
Abstract: Investigates the relationship between cheating and false excuse making to other forms of minor deviance. Clusters of deviant behaviors with factor analysis; Comparison of scores of cheaters and non-cheaters on measures of unreliability and risky driving behaviors; Prominence of false excuse makers on measures of substance abuse and illegal behaviors.

Title: Legal Cynicism and (Subcultural?) Tolerance of Deviance: The Neighborhood   Context of Racial Differences.
Source: Law & Society Review, 1998, Vol. 32 Issue 4, p777, 28p
Author(s): Sampson, Robert J.; Bartusch, Dawn Jeglum
Abstract: Presents a study on the sociodemographic and neighborhood sources of variation in tolerance of deviance, violence and attitudes about the legitimacy of law. Subcultural tolerance of deviance and violence; Anomie and legal cynicism;

Title: Cockfighting and backsliding: Deviance and postmodernism.
Source: Sociological Spectrum, Jul-Sep97, Vol. 17 Issue 3, p363, 11p
Author(s): Darden, Donna K.; Holyfield, Lori
Abstract: Presents a critique of postmodern theorizing through a narrative on cockfighting. Demonstration of the inconsistencies of the approach to postmodernism; Postmodern theorizing as a part of the process it critiques; Two questions arising from the deconstruction of the anecdote of cockfighting.

Practice Tests

Answers to these questions are found at the end of this manual.

Multiple Choice

1. Contributors to the upsurge in killings by teenagers in recent years include all of the following EXCEPT

    a. easy availability of guns.
    b. glamorization of violence in the movies, television, and video games.
    c. a culture that favors the possession of guns.
    d. easy availability of drugs and alcohol.

2. The fact that crime victims often unwittingly cooperate in the executive of a crime and that society is mostly indifferent is characteristics of what type of crime?

    a. street crime   c. corporate crime
    b. corporate crime   d. victimless crime

3. Women are more likely to suffer from depression and anxiety attacks while men tend to

    a. have antisocial personality and drug and alcohol abuse disorders.
    b. show distrust and resentment.
    c. have paranoid and sociopathic propensities.
    d. do not suffer from depression and anxiety attacks.

4. Which of Merton's five types of responses occurs when the goals are accepted but legitimate means to accomplish them are rejected?

    a. ritualism   c. innovation
    b. retreatism   d. rebellion

5. Homicide rates are generally higher for

    a. states who have abolished the death penalty.
    b. states who have retained the death penalty.
    c. states who have increased the number of prison beds.
    d. states who have increased financial support for police.

C 6. Which of the following statements represents a popular myth about women and rape?

    a. Most men believe that women fear and hate rape.
    b. Women who are raped are mostly seen as victims.
    c. Women have an unconscious wish to be raped.
    d. America is a rape-prone culture.

B 7. Attachment to conventional people and institutions, and a belief in the moral validity of rules are two ways we

    a. experience anomie.
    b. bond ourselves to society.
    c. suffer from the exploitation of the wealthy.
    d. become career deviants.

C 8. Power – or the lack of it – largely determines

    a. whether deviance occurs.
    b. whether crime occurs.
    c. what type of crime people is likely to commit.
    d. who becomes a criminal.

A 9. The heterogeneous and impersonal nature of modern society has created the need for more

    a. formal social controls.   c. accurate FBI statistics.
    b. informal social controls   d. sociological theories.

D 10. Which of the following kinds of deviance has recently become a fast-growing global industry that is caused by poverty and exploitation by rich countries?

    a. organized crime   c. mental illness
    b. homosexuality   d. prostitution

Fill In The Blank

1. _Anomie_ is a social condition in which norms are absent, weak, or in conflict.

2. Philip grew up in a broken family, and therefore did not develop a strong set of norms. Consequently, when he had trouble getting a job, he found other means to get money. Merton would categorize this type of deviant as an _innovator_

3. _Phenomenological_ theory is useful for understanding the subjective world of deviants.

4. If someone takes on a deviant identity and other people then see him or her as deviant, that person might take on a deviant _career_.

5. Drug use, truancy and drunkenness are considered to be nonpredatory types of _victimless_ deviant acts.

True or False

_F_ 1. Most murder victims are killed by strangers.

_F_ 2. Men with little or no sexual experience are more likely to be rapists.

_T_ 3. Overall, drug use in the United States has declined since the late 1970s.

_F_ 4 Strain theory assumes that women who have a strong desire for economic success but no opportunity to reach success are likely to commit a crime.

_F_ 5. Shaming theory suggests that disintegrative shaming is more effective in controlling deviance than reintegrative shaming.

Essay

1. Identify the attitudes toward women that could make men more prone to commit rape. Why is the victim of rape often portrayed as a willing partner?

2. Identify and explain the reasons corporate criminals use to maintain a noncriminal image. How do victims unwittingly cooperate with the corporate criminal?

3. Identify the four positive functions of *deviance* and explain how each appears to benefit society.

4. Using Merton's *strain theory*, identify the five responses of people to the dysfunctions between goals and means. What is the resulting deviance for each response?

5. Define *shaming* and describe the two types of shaming. Why could reintegrative shaming reduce crime in our society?

Chapter 6 Page 151 Anomie	Chapter 6 Page 143 Deviance
Chapter 6 Page 155 Differential Association	Chapter 6 Page 152 Disintegrative Shaming
Chapter 6 Page 154 Marginal Surplus Population	Chapter 6 Page 164 Medicalization of Deviance
Chapter 6 Page 149 Neurosis	Chapter 6 Page 157 Primary Deviance

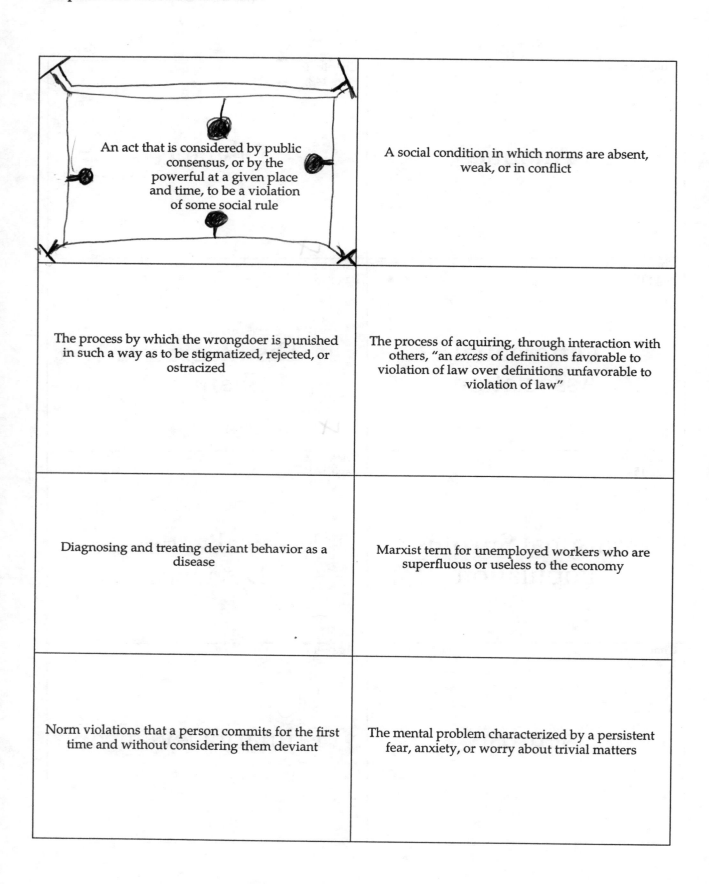

An act that is considered by public consensus, or by the powerful at a given place and time, to be a violation of some social rule

A social condition in which norms are absent, weak, or in conflict

The process by which the wrongdoer is punished in such a way as to be stigmatized, rejected, or ostracized

The process of acquiring, through interaction with others, "an *excess* of definitions favorable to violation of law over definitions unfavorable to violation of law"

Diagnosing and treating deviant behavior as a disease

Marxist term for unemployed workers who are superfluous or useless to the economy

Norm violations that a person commits for the first time and without considering them deviant

The mental problem characterized by a persistent fear, anxiety, or worry about trivial matters

Chapter 6 Page 149 Psychosis	Chapter 6 Page 144 Rape
Chapter 6 Page 152 Content Analysis	Chapter 6 Page 154 Relative Deprivation 4
Chapter 6 Page 157 4 Secondary Deviance	

Coercive sex that involves the use of force to get a woman to do something sexual against her will	The mental problem typified by loss of touch with reality
Feeling unable to achieve relatively high aspirations	Making wrongdoers feel guilty while showing them understanding, forgiveness, or even respect
	Repeated norm violations that the violators recognize as deviant

Chapter 7: U.S. and Global Stratification

Learning Objectives

After reading Chapter 7, the student should be able to:

1.   Define social stratification.
2.   Describe the three bases of stratification.
3.   Describe stratification systems around the world.
4.   Outline two new approaches to stratification.
5.   Identify social classes and use them to analyze the U.S. class structure and the influence of class.
6.   Analyze the nature and causes of poverty and homelessness in the U.S. and how the welfare systems helps or hinders the poor.
7.   Understand the determinants and patterns of social mobility.
8.   Explore some of the global patterns of stratification systems.
9.   Explore the question "Is stratification necessary?" through analysis and comparison of three perspectives on stratification, and describe ways to achieve social equality.
10.   Explore the emergence of stratification in cyberspace as presented in the "Sociological Frontiers" box.
11.   Study how persons have become millionaires as described in the "Using Sociology" box.

Key Concepts

absolute poverty
caste system
class system
dependency theory
feminization of poverty
horizontal mobility
individual mobility
intergenerational mobility
intragenerational mobility
Kuznets curve
life chances
life-styles
neocolonialism

objective method
power
power elite
relative poverty
reputational method
social class
social mobility
social stratification
status inconsistency
status system
structural mobility
subjective method
vertical mobility

Content Select Articles

[Note: The following articles are available to students through ContentSelect, a data base of sociological articles that students can use through purchase of the text. They can be found in the data base by typing in the author's name.]

Title: Toward a Broader Conceptual Framework for Research on Social Stratification, Childrearing Patterns, and Media Effects.
Source: Mass Communication & Society, Apr2001, Vol. 4 Issue 2
Author(s): Gaziano, Cecilie
Abstract: A theoretical framework describes differences in the social distribution of family childrearing patterns as a primary component in children's preferences for violent media content as well as a component in development of knowledge gaps and citizen participation differentials. The interrelated elements include family childrearing prototypes, attachment theory, authoritarian personality theory, and Kohn's (1976, 1977) theory of childrearing values. The concept of power underlies these elements on the levels of individuals, families, and society, as operationalized in (a) the perceptions of self-efficacy or powerlessness that the attachment process fosters in children; (b) parent-child power relations; and (c) ultimately, social power. Children of parents who feel powerless and who attempt to assert power through authoritarianism often grow up to have the same sense of powerlessness and other authoritarian characteristics

Title: Class analysis from a normative perspective.
Source: British Journal of Sociology, Dec2000, Vol. 51 Issue 4, p663, 17p, 1 graph
Author(s): Swift, Adam
Abstract: Distinguishing between an explanatory and a normative interest in social stratification, this paper considers the relation between class analysis and the value of equality. Starting from the familiar distinction between (in) equality of position and (in) equality of opportunity, and noting the extent to which mobility research focuses on the latter, it suggests that class positions can themselves be characterized in terms of the opportunities they yield to those occupying them. This enables the clear identification of the kinds of inequality that are and are not addressed by research findings presented in terms of class categories and odds ratios. The significance of those findings from a normative perspective is then discussed, and their limitations are emphasized - though the paper also explains in what ways they are indeed of normative relevance.

Title: Local capitalism, civic engagement, and socioeconomic well-being.
Source: Social Forces, Dec98, Vol. 77 Issue 2, p401, 28p, 6 charts
Author(s): Tolbert, Charles M.; Lyson, Thomas A.; Irwin, Michael D.
Abstract: Analyzes emerging body of social stratification research grounded in theories of civil society, local capitalism and civic engagement. Assumption that local capitalism and civic engagement are associated with positive socioeconomic development; Outline of needed research on civil society that would further contribute to social development.

Practice Tests

Answers to these questions are found at the end of this manual.

Multiple Choice

_____ 1. A stratification system where people are stratified according to their social prestige is called a _____ system.

    a. free enterprise   c. caste
    b. status   d. egalitarian

_____ 2. For sociologists, a society is stratified when

    a. the different classes of society struggle over scarce resources.
    b. persons with scarce resources have a high rank, and those without them are not included in the stratification system.
    c. persons with scarce resources have a high rank and those without them have a lower rank.
    d. scarce resources are distributed to everyone equally.

_____ 3. The amount of social inequality in a society depends on its

    a. economic development.   c. majority development.
    b. minority development.   d. class development.

_____ 4. A system in which people are stratified according to their social prestige is called a _____ system.

    a. caste   c. status
    b. political   d. feudal

_____ 5. Self-reporting and self-rating are important to the _____ method of identifying social class.

    a. survey   c. subjective
    b. reputational   d. ethnographic

_____ 6. Which of the following is characteristic of the middle class?

    a. home ownership and a comfortable life.
    b. a narrow range of occupational types
    c. not much college education
    d. low level, white-collar jobs

_____ 7. Liberals are opposed to providing federal funding to religious groups to assist the poor because

   a. it would compromise the group's religious mission.
   b. it would weaken the constitutional separation of church and state.
   c. it would provide religious groups the opportunity to convert more people to their beliefs.
   d. it would strengthen the constitutional separation of church and state.

_____ 8. Life style refers to

   a. tastes and preferences in daily living.
   b. tastes and preferences of famous people.
   c. opportunities available to individuals in their lives.
   d. the typical way of living that most people adopt.

_____ 9. Many sociologists argue that efforts to count the homeless are inaccurate because

   a. most persons who are homeless really have places to live.
   b. government studies fail to count the hidden homeless.
   c. the government does not have an adequate definition of homelessness.
   d. the government purposely undercounts the homeless.

_____ 10. Consequences of global inequality includes a higher prevalence of child exploitation through work partnerships with parents, children being forced to work outside the home and

   a. children being old or leased as slaves by parents.
   b. families having too many children.
   c. children being forced to attend school.
   d. children being forced to leave home at an early age.

Fill In The Blank

1. According to Karl Marx, the two social classes are the bourgeoisie and the _____.

2. A _____ system in a society is when some people are held as someone else's property.

3. The _____ class is made up of the old rich, or those families who have been rich for several generations.

4. Sources of structural mobility in the United States include expansion of industry, increase of educational levels, lower birth raters in the upper classes and the _____.

5. _____ in poor countries have fewer opportunities for paid employment.

True or False

_____ 1. Hunter-gathers tend to be egalitarian primarily because there is not an opportunity for individuals to accumulate wealth.

_____ 2. Although the upper class in the United States is only 3-5% of the total population, the upper class possess over 75% of America's wealth.

_____ 3. In general, the higher one's social class the more conservative they are on economic issues but are more liberal on social issues.

_____ 4. women as a group are less vulnerable than men to poverty because of the patriarchal nature of our society.

_____ 5. From a global perspective, the consequences of inequality can be seen through child exploitation, slavery, and disadvantages for women.

Essay

1. Summarize the characteristics of the major *social classes* in American society.

2. Define *feminization of poverty*. Why are women more vulnerable to poverty than men?

3. Summarize the function of *poverty*. Provide examples.

4. Identify the characteristics of *homeless* people. How are today's homeless different from those of years ago?

5. Identify popular beliefs about people on *welfare* and explain why these beliefs are untrue.

Chapter 7 Page 184 Absolute Poverty	Chapter 7 Page 177 Caste System
Chapter 7 Page 177 Class System	Chapter 7 Page 195 Dependency Theory
Chapter 7 Page 185 Feminization of Poverty	Chapter 7 Page 188 Horizontal Mobility
Chapter 7 Page 191 Individual Mobility	Chapter 7 Page 188 Intergenerational Mobility

A relatively rigid stratification system in which people's positions are ascribed and fixed	The lack of minimum food and shelter necessary for maintaining life
The theory that rich nations exploit poor ones for power and commercial gain, thereby perpetuating poverty, underdevelopment, and dependency on rich nations	A relatively open stratification system in which people's positions are achieved and changeable
Movement from one job to another within the same status ctegory	A huge number of women bearing the burden of poverty, mostly as single mothers or heads of families
A change in social standing from one generation to the next	Social mobility related to an individual's personal achievement and characteristics

Chapter 7 Page 188 Intragenerational Mobility	Chapter 7 Page 177 Kuznets Curve
Chapter 7 Page 183 Life Chances	Chapter 7 Page 183 Lifestyles
Chapter 7 Page 195 Neocolonialism	Chapter 7 Page 180 Objective Method
Chapter 7 Page 173 Power	Chapter 7 Page 174 Power Elite

The changing relationship between economic development and social inequality, named after its discoverer, Simon Kuznet	A change in an individual's social standing
Tastes, preferences, and ways of living	The likelihood of living a good, long, successful life in society
The method of identifying social classes using occupation, income, and education to rank people	The economic control exercised rich nations over their former colonies
A small group of top leaders, not just from business corporations but also from the federal government and the military	The ability to control the behavior of others, even against their will

Chapter 7 Page 185 Relative Poverty	Chapter 7 Page 180 Reputational Method
Chapter 7 Page 180 Social Class	Chapter 7 Page 188 Social Mobility
Chapter 7 Page 172 Social Stratification	Chapter 7 Page 175 Status Inconsistency
Chapter 7 Page 174 Status System	Chapter 7 Page 189 Structural Mobility

The method of identifying social classes by selecting a group of people and asking them to rank others

A state of deprivation resulting from having less than the majority of the people have

Movement from one social standing to another

A category of people who have about the same amount of income, power, and prestige

The condition in which the same individual is given two conflicting status rankings

The system in which some people get more or fewer rewards than others

Social mobility related to changes in society

A system in which people are stratified according to their social prestige

Chapter 7 Page 180 Subjective Method	Chapter 7 Page 188 Vertical Mobility

Moving up or down the status ladder	The method of identifying social classes by asking people to rank themselves

Chapter 8: Race and Ethnicity

Learning Objectives

After reading Chapter 8, the student should be able to:

1.   Describe how the 9/11 terrorist attack led to increased prejudice and discrimination against Arab-Americans.
2.   List the major ways in which people are identified as racial and/or ethnic minorities and state the sociological definition of a minority group.
3.   Recount the experiences of major U.S. minority groups, including African-Americans, Hispanics, and Asians.
4.   Use the three sociological perspectives to describe patterns of racial and ethnic relations.
5.   Define and analyze some causes of prejudice and discrimination, and efforts like affirmative action to change them.
6.   Understand race relations from a global perspective.

Key Concepts

affirmative action
amalgamation
anti-Semitism
assimilation
behavioral assimilation
cultural pluralism
de facto segregation
de jure segregation
discrimination
ethnic group
genocide

glass ceiling
institutionalized discrimination
Jim Crow Laws
minority
prejudice
race
racism
scapegoating
stereotype
structural assimilation

Content Select Articles

[Note: The following articles are available to students through ContentSelect, a data base of sociological articles that students can use through purchase of the text. They can be found in the data base by typing in the author's name.]

Title: Affirmative action in a global perspective: The cases of South Africa and Brazil.

Source: Sociological Spectrum, Oct-Dec99, Vol. 19 Issue 4, p443, 23p, 2 charts

Author(s): Guiilebeau, Christopher

Abstract: Most research on affirmative action is limited to the study of only one nation or country, typically the United States. In this article, I examine current and historical trends of affirmative action and racial preferences programs in a triangular perspective. From a *social* history of South Africa and Brazil, I develop a model of diversity achievement that compares these countries to theUnited States. Despite several significant problems, including the neglect of Black women, South Africa has achieved the most successful national policy of fair racial representation. Affirmative action is legally forbidden in Brazil, but growing protests and work by advocacy groups are slowly gaining the support of government officials. However, the existence of a complicated *social stratification* system based on skin color presents a difficult conundrum for the country's policymakers.

Title: Fitting into Categories or Falling Between Them? Rethinking ethnic classification.

Source: British Journal of Sociology of Education, Dec2000, Vol. 21 Issue 4, p487,

Author(s): Bonnett, Alastair; Carrington, Bruce

Abstract: The collection of ethnic and racial statistics has become common in a growing number of institutional settings. Yet contemporary approaches to *race* and *ethnicity* suggest that the very process of compelling people to assign themselves to one of a small number of racial or ethnic 'boxes' is, at best, essentialist and, at worst, racist. This article will explore this problematic terrain, and venture a pathway through it, with the aid of findings from a study of ethnic minority English and Welsh student teachers' attitudes to ethnic classification. The discussion comprises three parts. The first sets out to provide a brief theoretical analysis of the genesis of ethnic monitoring within the modern state. It is concluded that ethnic monitoring may usefully be regarded as a problematic necessity, a process that itself needs constant monitoring. With this agenda in place, we move on to assess the implications of our findings on student teachers' attitudes to ethnic monitoring. Their pointers for reform are discussed in the third and final section of the paper, where the policy implications of research are outlined.

Title: The Racial Canons of American Sociology: Identity Across the Lifespan as Biracial Alternative.

Source: American Sociologist, Spring2000, Vol. 31 Issue 1, p86, 8p

Author(s): Hall, Ronald E.

Abstract: The utilization of racial canons in American sociology has dictated traditional models of identity. Biracial Americans are consistently identified based upon the presumed *race* category of their African heritage. The result is that biracial Americans are ambiguous pertaining to racial identity without consideration of their lifespan experience, i.e.: social, cultural, and familial. To enable a more applicable model of identity will require that sociologists terminate the use of racial canons as a dictate of identity. Accordingly, development across the lifespan is heretofore both commensurate with biracial identity and the unique biracial experience.

Title: *Ethnicity* among Asians.
Source: Society, Nov/Dec98, Vol. 36 Issue 1, p6, 1/3p
Abstract: Discusses the cultural differences of specific ethnic groups in Asia. Ethnic groups evaluated; Racial treatments among Asians and Europeans; Significance of ethnic choices in culture.

Practice Tests

Answers to these questions are found at the end of this manual.

Multiple Choice

_____ 1. Even through people's physical characteristics do not change when they move to another part of the country, it is possible that their _____ classification may change.

    a. class   c. ethnic
    b. racial   d. economic

_____ 2. Sociologists use a societal definition of race because that helps them understand

    a. how racial groups share cultural features.
    b. why racial groups have a high level of interaction between their members.
    c. how societies use them to assign peoples to racial statuses.
    d. the scientific basis of racial categories.

_____ 3. Which one of the following statements reflects the essence of a minority group?

    a. Their members make up a small percentage of the population.
    b. Their members must have a weak sense of common identity.
    c. Membership is either ascribed or achieved.
    d. Their members experience prejudice and discrimination.

_____ 4. Which of the following is an example of discrimination?

    a. not hiring a person on the basis of race
    b. resenting people's success because of their ethnicity
    c. fearing people because of their race
    d. assuming that people's intelligence level is based on their ethnic background

_____ 5. Studies indicate that in the years since Congress passed the 1964 Civil Rights Act, there has been a significant decline in opposition to all of the following issues, EXCEPT for

    a. school integration.
    b. integrated housing.
    c. promotion of economic inequality.
    d. interracial marriage.

_____ 6. In 1954, the Supreme Court ordered America to

    a. desegregate its public schools.
    b. resegregate its public schools.
    c. desegregate housing and hotels.
    d. segregate housing and hotels.

_____ 7. The Chinese were brought to the U.S. as cheap labor to build railroads and dig mines. After these projects were complete, they were competing with white workers for jobs. As a result, all of the following EXCEPT were instituted to prohibit the Chinese from being equal with whites.

    a. owing property   c. seeking employment
    b. attending school   d. paying taxes

_____ 8. Even though segregation sanctioned by law has been abolished, segregation that is a result of tradition and custom still exists. Sociologists call this _____ segregation.

    a. dejure   c. traditional
    b. defacto   d. sanctioned

_____ 9. Prejudice and discrimination

    a. always occur together.
    b. do not necessarily go hand in hand.
    c. are likely to occur more often against people classified by race, rather than ethnicity.
    d. do not occur in agricultural societies.

_____ 10. The author of the text identifies several causes of prejudice and discrimination. Which of the following is NOT one of the causes identified?

    a. sociological   c. racism
    b. economic   d. political

Fill In The Blank

1. Because races have been inbred for thousands of years, there are no _____ races.

2. _____ refers to actions against other people on the basis of their group membership.

3. _____ Americans are more likely than white Americans to graduate from college and have a higher family income.

4. According to the _____ perspective, intergroup relations appear in the form of segregation, expulsion, and extermination.

5. _____ discrimination remains a major barrier to social equality although legal discrimination in the U.S. has ended.

True or False

_____ 1. In 1654, the first Jews came to the U.S. They came from Russia.

_____ 2. "White Ethics" refers to immigrants from Italy, Poland, Russia and other European countries.

_____ 3. the United States, more than most societies, is composed of one dominant ethnic group.

_____ 4. Most minorities consider assimilation necessary to become economically and socially acceptable.

_____ 5. Regardless of prejudice and discrimination, young victims tend to develop a positive self-image.

Essay

1. Define *prejudice* and *discrimination*. How does prejudice and discrimination create minority groups.

2. Identify the reasons the American government created Indian reservations. What were the consequences of this policy for the Indians?

3. Define *cultural pluralism* and *amalgamation*. How do these two patterns apply to American society?

4. Describe how the role of *socialization* in perpetuates *prejudice* and *discrimination*.

5. Identify some of the efforts the U.S. government has implement to combat prejudice and discrimination.

Chapter 8
Page 226

Affirmative Action

Chapter 8
Page 220

Amalgamation

Chapter 8
Page 217

Anti-Semitism

Chapter 8
Page 220

Assimilation

Chapter 8
Page 220

Behavioral Assimilation

Chapter 8
Page 220

Cultural Pluralism

Chapter 8
Page 222

De Facto Segregation

Chapter 8
Page 222

De Jure Segregation

The process by which the subcultures of various groups are blended together, forming a new culture	A policy that requires employers and academic institutions to make special efforts to recruit qualified minorities for jobs, promotions, and educational opportunities
The process by which a minority adopts the dominant group's culture as the culture of the larger society	Prejudice or discrimination against Jews
The peaceful coexistence of various racial and ethnic groups, each retaining its own subculture	The social situation in which a minority adopts the dominant group's language, values, and behavioral patterns
Segregation sanctioned by law	Segregation resulting from tradition and custom

Chapter 8 Page 209 Discrimination	Chapter 8 Page 208 Ethnic Group
Chapter 8 Page 222 Genocide	Chapter 8 Page 217 Glass Ceiling
Chapter 8 Page 224 Institutionalized Discrimination	Chapter 8 Page 211 Jim Crow Laws
Chapter 8 Page 209 Minority	Chapter 8 Page 209 Prejudice

A collection of people who share a distinctive cultural heritage	An unfavorable action against individuals that is taken because they are a member of a certain category
The prejudiced belief that keeps minority professionals from holding leadership positions in organizations	The wholesale killing of members of a specific racial or ethnic group
A set of laws that segregated African Americans from whites in all kinds of public and private facilities	The persistence of discrimination in social institutions that is not necessarily recognized by everyone as discrimination
A negative attitude toward a certain category of people	A racial or ethnic group that is subjected to prejudice and discrimination

Chapter 8 Page 207 Race	Chapter 8 Page 221 Racism
Chapter 8 Page 224 Scapegoating	Chapter 8 Page 222 Stereotype
Chapter 8 Page 220 Structural Assimilation	

The belief that one's own race or ethnicity is superior to that of others	A group of people who are perceived by a given society to be biologically different from others
An oversimplified, inaccurate mental picture of others	Blaming others for one's own failure
	The social condition in which the minority is accepted on equal terms with the rest of society

Chapter 9: Gender and Age

Learning Objectives

After reading Chapter 9, the student should be able to:

1. Define gender roles, compare U.S. conceptions of masculinity and femininity to those in other cultures, and explore origins of gender roles.
2. List and describe the different agents of gender socialization.
3. Describe the different spheres of gender inequalities, the role of sexism in rationalizing those inequalities, and the women's movement is fighting back.
4. Explore some of the consequences of gender inequality in both the U.S. and globally.
5. Analyze the three sociological perspectives on gender inequality.
6. Outline biological, psychological and social aspects of aging and study aging in other cultures.
7. Analyze how social class, gender and race and ethnicity contribute to the social diversity of aging.
8. Explore the future of aging.
9. Study gender differences in cyberspace games as presented in "Sociological Frontiers."
10. Study how to reduce gender inequality as described in the "Using Sociology" box.

Key Concepts

crystalline intelligence
expressive role
feminism
fluid intelligence
gender role
instrumental role

roleless role
senescence
senility
sexism
sexual harassment

Content Select Articles

[Note: The following articles are available to students through ContentSelect, a data base of sociological articles that students can use through purchase of the text. They can be found in the data base by typing in the author's name.]

Title:	The Formative Years: How Parenthood Creates *Gender*.
Source:	Canadian Review of Sociology & Anthropology, Nov2001, Vol. 38 Issue 4, p373, 18p
Abstract:	Presents findings from a study of heterosexual couples as they made the transition to parenthood. Changes of women's experiences after birth; Significant roles of a partner; Conventional division of labor at home.

Title: 'Seeing the Female Body Differently': *gender* issues in The Silence of the Lambs.

Source: Journal of Gender Studies, Nov2001, Vol. 10 Issue 3, p297, 14p

Author(s):   Dubois, Diane

Abstract: In this paper it is argued that the habitual representation of women in film has played a considerable part in constructing ideas of femininity, which contemporary filmmaking can deconstruct. The Silence of the Lambs deconstructs femininity as it has been constructed in four classic genres: the serial killer movie, the horror or monster movie, the 'pupil and mentor' movie and the 'psychiatrist and patient' movie. The Silence of the Lambs can be shown to deconstruct the generic amalgam of voyeurism, the 'male gaze' of the camera, castration anxiety and the confused and reinstated *gender* identities typical of the serial killer movie. The empathy between Doctor Hannibal 'the cannibal' Lecter and young FBI agent Clarice Starling criticises the encoding strategies of the classic monster movie wherein both woman and monster are feared objects within patriarchal orders of seeing. In psychiatrist and patient films, the heroine's behaviour is explainable when located within the patriarchal metanarrative of psychoanalysis, towards which The Silence of the Lambs is deeply ambivalent.

Title: Environment Through a Gendered Lens: From Person-in-Environment to Woman-in-Environment.

Source: Affilia: Journal of Women & Social Work, Spring2001, Vol. 16 Issue 1, p7, 24p,

Author(s):   Kemp, Susan P.

Abstract: Building on interdisciplinary work by critical and feminist scholars in geography, architecture and urban planning, and history, this article proposes a reworking of social work's person-environment formulation to incorporate *gender* and its implications more fully. Three interlocking domains are addressed: (a) women's subjective experiences of their everyday environments; (b) the connections among these environmental experiences, the geography of women's lives, and larger social categories such as race/ethnicity, class, and sexual orientation; and (c) women's environmental strengths, resources, and agency.

Title: Quality of life in the coming decades.

Source: Society, Jan/Feb99, Vol. 36 Issue 2, p56, 5p

Author(s):   Schwartz, Pepper

Abstract: Focuses on the issues about quality of life that are already foreseeable from trends. *Aging* and long-lived baby boom; Sacrelization of emotion; Socialization of children; Search for community; Conflict of generations; Future of sex education.

Title: Whence Comes Death?

Source: Humanist, Jan/Feb2002, Vol. 62 Issue 1, p24, 6p

Author(s):   Mitteldorf, Joshua

Abstract: Discusses the concept of *aging* and death in human beings. Idea of *aging* in developmental biology; Conception of *aging* by humanity; Explanation for an evolutionary reason for *aging* and death.

Practice Tests

Answers to these questions are found at the end of this manual.

Multiple Choice

_____ 1. Which of the following traits are associated with the traditional male gender role?

   a. passive   c. emotional and easy to cry
   b. easily intimidated   d. independent

_____ 2. Around the world,

   a. male dominance over women is nearly universal.
   b. women have attained a substantial degree of equality.
   c. women rarely suffer violence at the hands of men.
   d. women have about the same social positions as men.

_____ 3. Which of the following is true for boys rather than girls when involved with their same-sex peers?

   a. engagement in more cooperative kinds of play
   b. hanging around with a larger group of casual friends
   c. talking about the offense of others behind their backs
   d. learning cooperation, intimacy, and indirectness

_____ 4. Elementary and secondary school children are taught a subtle lesson of gender-role differences at school because

   a. women need men in leadership positions, such as principal.
   b. men hold positions of authority in schools while women serve in positions of subservience.
   c. men are more qualified to be principals and women are only quality to be teachers.
   d. men are needed to handle the incorrigibles.

_____ 5. Theoretically, women can acquire more political power than men because

   a. female voters outnumber male voters.
   b. women are better politicians than men.
   c. men tend not to vote.
   d. women campaign more vigorously than men.

_____ 6. According to research, a large majority of females today

    a. believe that the feminist movement is outdated.
    b. believe that being feminine is important.
    c. believe that there is not a conflict between being a feminist and being feminine.
    d. believe that society should return to patriarchy.

_____ 7. According to the author of the text, more than half of all college women

    a. enjoy an active sexual life.
    b. have been sexually assaulted by their dates.
    c. are sexually active with only one partner.
    d. do not engage in sexual activity.

_____ 8. An example of social aging is

    a. the onset of diabetes.
    b. memory loss.
    c. enhanced feelings of self-worth.
    d. retirement from one's job.

_____ 9. Older people have lost status in many industrial societies because

    a. their skills became obsolete.
    b. they were replaced by machines.
    c. people moved to urban areas.
    d. they earned less money than younger individuals.

_____ 10. Which of the following is one reason why elderly women suffer financially?

    a. Women's work is not as valuable to society as men's work.
    b. Women are not eligible for social security benefits.
    c. More women have been dependent on their husbands' earnings.
    d. Few women work.

Fill In The Blank

1. _____ are about how men and women behave and expectations are about how they should behave.

2. What makes one person female and another person male has to do with their _____.

3. The "third wave" of feminism has caused women to reach out and work with _____.

4. _____ is an abnormal condition characterized by loss of memory, confusion, and loss of ability to reason.

5. Stereotypes of the elderly, such as their being rigid, forgetful, and unproductive, reinforce _____ against the elderly.

True or False

_____ 1. In a traditional society, women are expected to be rational, intuitive, and objective.

_____ 2. Male dominance over females is almost universal.

_____ 3. Women's magazines still tend to address women's issues from a traditional gender-role perspective.

_____ 4. Biological and psychological aging affects people in the same ways, especially with the intervention of social factors.

_____ 5. Older African Americans suffer from the effects of racial discrimination to a greater extent than younger African Americans.

Essay

1. Explain the role of the *family* in socializing children into a specific gender role. How has this socialization changed in recent years?

2. Explain how the mass media perpetuates *gender stereotypes*, especially for women. Do you see any changes occurring in how the mass media presents women's roles today? Explain.

3. Define *sexism* and explain how it promotes inequality and discrimination.

4. Define *ageism* and explain how the elderly are discriminated against.

5. Define a *roleless* role. How to the elderly often become trapped in this role?

Chapter 9 Page 256 Crystalline Intelligence	Chapter 9 Page 253 Expressive Role
Chapter 9 Page 248 Feminism	Chapter 9 Page 256 Fluid Intelligence
Chapter 9 Page 236 Gender Role	Chapter 9 Page 253 Instrumental Role
Chapter 9 Page 259 Roleless Role	Chapter 9 Page 255 Senescence

A role that requires taking care of personal relationships	Wisdom and insight into the human condition, as shown by one's skills in language, philosophy, music, or painting
The ability to grasp abstract relationships, as in mathematics, physics, or some other science	The belief that women and men should be equal in various aspects of their lives
A role that requires performance of a task	The pattern of attitudes and behaviors that a society expects of its members because of their being female or male
An abnormal condition characterized by serious memory loss, confusion, and loss of the ability to reason	The natural physical process of aging

Chapter 9
Page 242

Sexism

Chapter 9
Page 250

Sexual Harassment

An unwelcome act of a sexual nature	Prejudice and discrimination based on one's gender

Chapter 10: Families

Learning Objectives

After reading Chapter 10, the student should be able to:

1. State why the traditional image of the family no longer describes American families.
2. Understand the family from a global view, including patterns of mate selection and authority.
3. State the functional, conflict and symbolic interactionist perspectives on the family, and use them to describe the American family.
4. Describe the American process of meeting, marriage and divorce.
5. Analyze the family problems of violence and divorce.
6. Analyze some of the changes in the American family, including the emergence of single-parent families, living together, and blended families.
7. Examine the life-styles that are alternatives to the family such as staying single and living together.
8. Understand the social diversity of U.S. families.
9. Explore the future of the family.
10. Study the revival of covenant marriages, as presented in the Sociological Frontiers box.
11. Examine ways of solving marital problems as presented in the Using Sociology box.

Key Concepts

arranged marriage
bilateral descent
egalitarian family
endogamy
exogamy
extended family
family of orientation
family of procreation
homogamy
matriarchal family
matrilineal descent

matrilocal residence
monogamy
neolocal residence
nuclear family
patriarchal family
patrilineal descent
patrilocal residence
polyandry
polygamy
polygyny
serial monogamy

Content Select Articles

[Note: The following articles are available to students through ContentSelect, a data base of sociological articles that students can use through purchase of the text. They can be found in the data base by typing in the author's name.]

Title: Families and Self-Sacrifice: Alternative Models and Meanings for Family Theory.

Source: Social Forces, Jun2001, Vol. 79 Issue 4, p1231, 28p

Author(s):   Bahr, Howard M.; Bahr, Kathleen S.

Abstract: The concept of sacrifice used to be a dominant theme in social scientific theorizing, but it is now so neglected that recent work speaks of the need for a "recovery" of sacrifice. Similarly, self-sacrifice in the service of family members, formerly seen as high virtue, is now often characterized as personality defect or self-defeating behavior. Neither self-sacrifice nor family love play a significant part in the prevailing family theories, grounded as they are in the assumption of self-interest and framed in the logic of utilitarian individualism and the rationalized marketplace. This "silence" is more ideologically based than reflective of family process. The absence of a language of sacrifice and love limits our ability to give voice to our experience, and the professional neglect of these concepts diminishes our understanding of the processes they name. Some recent work on sacrifice by scholars in other disciplines has implications for family theory. We draw from the disciplines of economics, history, philosophy, literature, sociology, and from life as lived by everyday people in making the case that self-sacrifice is a powerful and essential part of social life generally, and family life in particular.

Title: Assortative Meeting and Mating: unintended Consequences of Organized Settings for Partner Choices.

Source: Social Forces, Jun2001, Vol. 79 Issue 4, p1289, 24p

Author(s):   Kalmijn, Matthijs; Flap, Henk

Abstract: An important hypothesis about why people generally interact with people who are socially or culturally similar to themselves is that the opportunities they have to meet similar others are greater than the opportunities they have to meet dissimilar others. We examine this supply-side perspective on social relationships by empirically linking marriage choices to the type of setting couples had in common before they married. We focus on five meeting settings (work, school, the neighborhood, common family networks, and voluntary associations) and five types of homogamy (with respect to age, education, class destinations, class origins, and religious background). Using data from face-to-face interviews among married and cohabiting couples in the Netherlands, we show that these five contexts account for a sizable portion of the places where partners have met.

Title: SOCIAL SCIENCE FINDINGS AND THE 'FAMILY WARS.'

Source: Society, May/Jun2001, Vol. 38 Issue 4, p13, 7p

Author(s):   Glenn, Norval D.

Abstract: Focuses on the relationship between social science and ideology in family issues in the United States. Components of ideology; Kinds of values;

Complications for the assessment of derivative values; Misuses of family social science findings; Constructive and inappropriate uses of social science findings.

Title: Dual-earner families in Finland: differences between and within families in relation to work and family experiences.
Source: Community, Work & Family, Apr2001, Vol. 4 Issue 1, 4 charts, 1 graph
Author(s):   Kinnunen, Ulla; Mauno, Saija
Abstract: Focuses on the typology of dual-earner families in Finland. Differences between the families in family functioning and work-family interface experiences; Interpretations of the between-group and within-parent differences in the clustering variables; Link between job exhaustion and problems in family functioning.

Practice Tests

Answers to these questions are found at the end of this manual.

Multiple Choice

_____ 1. John and Janet married and had two children, Joe and Jill. With their children, John and Janet form a (n)

   a. family of orientation.
   b. family of procreation.
   c. extended family.
   d. communal family.

_____ 2. Blood ties are stronger than marital bonds in _____ societies.

   a. patrilocal   c. modern
   b. industrialized   d. traditional

_____ 3. The most pervasive type of family found in the world where the oldest male is head of the family is called a _____ family.

   a. matriarcal   c. communal
   b. egalitarian   d. patriarcal

_____ 4. Western societies have traditionally been restrictive with regard to sexual norms, tying sex to marriage. The author of the text suggests that this appears to serve all of the following functions, EXCEPT

    a. giving people the incentive to marry.
    b. minimizing sexual competition.
    c. preventing divorce.
    d. ensuring children will be well cared for.

_____ 5. Which of the following is NOT a basic function of the family?

    a. socialization   c. differentiation
    b. reproduction   d. emotional support

_____ 6. People in traditional societies spurn romantic love and believe it is more rational to marry someone of good character and for _____.

    a. economic security.   c. personal growth.
    b. children.   d. a nice home.

_____ 7. When asked, most Americans report that their marriages are

    a. full of conflict.   c. successful.
    b. satisfactory.   d. overwhelmingly happy.

_____ 8. Many battered women do not leave their husbands, even when they continue to receive abuse. Two reasons for this is because they are economically isolated and they

    a. fear they will lose their children.
    b. fear retaliation from their husbands.
    c. fear they will kill their husbands.
    d. fear they will be killed by their husbands.

_____ 9. Many experts feel that a high divorce rate means that

    a. the American institution of marriage is strong.
    b. the American institution of marriage is weak.
    c. marriage is no longer a relevant commitment.
    d. marriage rates will become lower in the future.

_____ 10. Dual-career families are different from two-paycheck families in that

    a. in dual-career families both husband and wife have careers.
    b. in two-paycheck families, both husband and wife maintain separate budgets.
    c. dual-career families have more children.
    d. dual-career families will choose to have children even if it disrupts their careers.

Fill In The Blank

1. In many traditional societies parents select partners for their children. This type of marriage is called _____.

2. The _____ function of the family prohibits sexual intercourse between close relatives.

3. The _____ ritual developed in the United States at the end of world War I and has spread to other industrial countries.

4. One of the five social forces behind the higher divorce rate today in the United States is decreased social _____.

5. According to sociologists, cohabitation is not the reason there is a high divorce rate for persons who cohabitate prior to marriage. They believe the main reason for the high divorce rate in this group is _____.

True or False

_____ 1. A conjugal family is one in which relatives from several generations live together.

_____ 2. When Jake and Sally married they moved into a new home of their own. This is called neolocal residence by sociologists.

_____ 3. The regulation of sexuality has become an increasingly important function of the family.

_____ 4. Tim and Sally are a married couple who basically agree on major issues, enjoy the same activities and express affection for each other. Sociologists would say they have a successful marriage.

_____ 5. Since the early 1990s, the number of unmarried teenage mothers has risen sharply.

Essay

1. Describe why some societies view *arranged marriages* as better suited for their members than America's view of marriage through romantic love.

2. Identify four of the factors that researchers have found present in successful marriages. Do you agree or disagree with these factors? Why or why not?

3. Identify reasons why *domestic violence occurs*. Explain why it is difficult to measure domestic violence.

4. Identify the reasons why some people choose to stay single rather than marry. What is the attitude of these singles toward marriage.

5. Identify why researchers believe that the family is NOT going away. How might the family look in the future?

Chapter 10 Page 267 Arranged Marriage	Chapter 10 Page 268 Bilateral Descent
Chapter 10 Page 268 Egalitarian Family	Chapter 10 Page 268 Endogamy
Chapter 10 Page 26 Exogamy	Chapter 10 Page 266 Extended Family
Chapter 10 Page 266 Family of Orientation	Chapter 10 Page 266 Family of Procreation

The norm that recognizes both parents' families as the child's close relatives	The norm that recognizes both parents' families as the child's close relatives
Literally, "marrying within," the act of marrying someone from one's own group	The family in which authority is equally distributed between husband and wife
The family that consists of two parents, their unmarried children, and other relatives	Literally, "marrying outward," the act of marrying someone from outside one's group—such as the clan, tribe, or village
The family that one establishes through marriage, consisting of oneself and one's spouse and children	The family in which one grows up, consisting of oneself and one's parents and siblings

Chapter 10 Page 273 Homogamy	Chapter 10 Page 268 Matriarchal Family
Chapter 10 Page 268 Matrilineal Descent	Chapter 10 Page 268 Matrilocal Residence
Chapter 10 Page 268 Monogamy	Chapter 1 Page 268 Neolocal Residence
Chapter 10 Page 266 Nuclear Family	Chapter 10 Page 268 Patriarchal Family

The family in which the dominant figure is the oldest female	Marrying someone with social characteristics similar to one's own
The home where the married couple lives with the wife's family	The norm that recognizes only the mother's family as a child's close relatives
The home where the married couple live by themselves, away from both the husband's and the wife's families	The marriage of one man to one woman
The family in which the dominant figure is the oldest male	The family that consists of two parents and their unmarried children

Chapter 10
Page 268

Patrilineal Descent

Chapter 10
Page 268

Patrilocal Residence

Chapter 10
Page 268

Polyandry

Chapter 10
Page 268

Polygamy

Chapter 10
Page 268

Polygyny

Chapter 10
Page 268

Serial Monogamy

The home where the married couple live with the husband's family	The norm that recognizes only the father's family as a child's close relatives
The marriage of one person to two or more people of the opposite sex	The marriage of one woman to two or more men
The marriage of one person to two or more people but one at a time	The marriage of one man to two or more women

Chapter 11: Education and Religion

Learning Objectives

After reading Chapter 11, the student should be able to:

1. Describe several ways Americans pursue education and religious experience.
2. Outline the three sociological perspectives on education.
3. Summarize some features of education in the United States, including the problems faced by the schools and new educational developments.
4. Describe social diversity in U.S. education.
5. Outline the three sociological perspectives on religion.
6. Analyze religion in the United States, including religious affiliation, social diversity and the fundamentalist revival.
7. Understand the problems many religions face when they must deal with the secular world.
8. Undertake a global analysis of religion.
9. Explore the "Sociological Frontier" of understanding religious fundamentalism and terrorism.
10. Outline the secrets of doing well in college, as described in the Using Sociology section on "How to Make It in College."

Key Concepts

animism
church
civil religion
compensatory education
cult
cultural imperialism
ethicalism
monotheism

polytheism
pygmalion effect
sect
shamanism
theism
totemism
tracking

Content Select Articles

[Note: The following articles are available to students through ContentSelect, a data base of sociological articles that students can use through purchase of the text. They can be found in the data base by typing in the author's name.]

Title: Race, Religion, and Religious Involvement: A Comparative Study of Whites and African Americans.
Source: Social Forces, Dec2001, Vol. 80 Issue 2, p605, 27p
Author(s):   Hunt, Larry L.; Hunt, Matthew O.
Abstract: This research examines (1) whether a comparative study of African Americans and whites in a nationwide sample bears out the widespread assumption of a distinctive African American religiosity (when region and other factors are controlled), and (2) whether any race differences provide support for the "semi-involuntary" interpretation of African American religious involvements. Using data from the 1974-94 General Social Surveys, we examine how a variety of qualifying the assertion of a generalized heightened religiosity.

Title: Religious Involvement, Stress, and Mental Health: Findings from the 1995 Detroit Area Study.
Source: Social Forces, Sep2001, Vol. 80 Issue 1, p215, 35p
Author(s):   Ellison, Christopher G.; Boardman, Jason D.; Williams, David R.; Jackson, James S.
Abstract: Although interest in the links between religion and mental health has increased sharply in recent years, researchers remain far from a consensus regarding which aspects of religious involvement are germane to mental health, which mental health outcomes may be influenced by religious factors, and which mechanisms and/or models may account for these observed relationships. This article extends the literature in this area by elaborating a set of direct, mediating, and moderating links between multiple dimensions of religious involvement and psychological distress and well-being.

Title: God, Politics, and Protest: Religious Beliefs and the Legitimation of Contentious Tactics.
Source: Social Forces, Jun2001, Vol. 79 Issue 4, p1425, 34p
Author(s):   McVeigh, Rory; Sikkink, David
Abstract: Most students of social protest now agree that protest participation and participation in institutionalized politics are both potentially effective means of addressing individual and collective grievances. A primary conceptual distinction between the two forms of political participation centers on the contentious nature of protest. We focus attention on the disruptive potential of religious beliefs and values and argue that approval of contentious tactics is a critical link between religious beliefs and protest participation. We analyze data from a representative sample of churchgoing Protestants in the United States.

Title: The School Class as an Interaction Order.
Source: British Journal of Sociology of Education, Jun2001, Vol. 22 Issue 2, p267, 11p
Author(s):   Vanderstraeten, Raf
Abstract: Drawing on the works of Erving Goffman and Niklas Luhmann, it is argued that face-to-face interactions establish realities sui generis. They have a life on their own, and make demands on their own behalf. They are able to constitute their own boundaries by means of an intricate interplay of processes of reflective perception and communication. Even an organizational setting cannot determine this interaction order; it can only change the conditions within which interaction takes place. Against this theoretical background, this article analyzes the basic characteristics of the organizationally framed interaction order of classroom education. It also sketches perspectives for empirical and historical research on educational interaction in the school class.

Practice Tests

Answers to these questions are found at the end of this manual.

Multiple Choice

_____ 1. The most obvious function of education is to

    a. provide a place for the custody of children.
    b. give needy students free lunch and a variety of programs.
    c. provide a new generation with knowledge and skills.
    d. provide secure jobs for otherwise unskilled employees.

_____ 2. The conflict perspective argues that elementary and secondary schools train

    a. upper class children to respect authority.
    b. lower class children to respect authority and obey orders.
    c. lower class children to exercise responsibility and independence.
    d. lower class children to use skills necessary to enter middle level professions and occupations.

_____ 3. Teacher unions are opposed to the school voucher plans for all of the following reasons, EXCEPT

    a. encourages school choice based on racial or ethnic prejudice.
    b. takes the government funding away from poor schools.
    c. would greatly improve poor schools.
    d. violates the principle of separation of church and state.

_____ 4. A compensatory program that evidently produces only temporary gains in the academic achievement of disadvantaged children is

a. Project Remediation.
b. student work study.
c. cultural inclusion activities.
d. Project Head Start.

_____ 5. The "unschooling" type of home-based curricula emphasizes

a. freedom for children to pursue their interest with parents providing resources and guidance.
b. Parents "undoing" what public schools have taught.
c. Freedom for parents to pursue whatever educational avenues they choose.
d. Freedom for students to choose if they want to go to school or not.

_____ 6. If religion offers too much support and consolation, it can

a. become too institutionalized.
b. impede social change.
c. further reckless or revolutionary social change.
d. lead to mixed motivations.

_____ 7. Among churchgoers in the United States, very few attend services

a. because of peer or community pressure.
b. to find friends.
c. to make social connections.
d. for strictly religious reasons.

_____ 8. According to his students on cults, Sam Levine found that many young people join cults

a. as a transition from family.
b. as an escape from peers.
c. as a transition from one religion to another.
d. as an escape from drugs and crime.

_____ 9. The higher an individual's social class, the

a. less likely he will attend church regularly.
b. more likely he will be emotionally involved in the religion.
c. more likely he will attend church regularly.
d. less likely he will seek leadership positions in the church.

_____ 10. When a church becomes successful, it faces a series of dilemmas. Which of the following statements is NOT a feeling of security and power that an established religion creates?

    a. the dilemma of mixed motivation
    b. the dilemma of administrative order
    c. the dilemma of powerlessness
    d. the symbolic dilemma

Fill In The Blank

1. A major latent function of education is _____ care.

2. City schools that need to be integrated lure white families back to the city by offering special science and language classes. These schools are called _____ schools.

3. The _____ function of religion enables an individual to know who they are and the purpose of their life.

4. The Unification Church is an example of a large _____.

5. _____ is a type of religion that centers on the worship of a god or gods.

True or False

_____ 1. U.S. high school students score higher on science and math tests than Japanese students.

_____ 2. Charter schools are part of the public school system and offer specialized subjects for students.

_____ 3. Durkheim believed religion helped maintain society.

_____ 4. People who join cults generally come from religious, traditional families.

_____ 5. There is a strict separation of church and state in the United States and when asked, people indicate they believe it should remain separated.

Essay

1. Identify the functions of *education*. Are these functions still important today? Why or why not?

2. Define *cultural imperialism*. How does this impact education?

3. Define *lifelong learning* and describe how it occurs.

4. Identify the functions of *religion*. What relationship did Durkheim see between religion and society?

5. Identify the three major forms of religion around the world. What are the major differences in these three forms?

Chapter 11 Page 319 Animism	Chapter 11 Page 315 Church
Chapter 11 Page 317 Civil Religion	Chapter 11 Page 298 Compensatory Education
Chapter 11 Page 311 Cult	Chapter 11 Page 295 Cultural Imperialism
Chapter 11 Page 319 Ethicalism	Chapter 11 Page 319 Monotheism

A relatively large, well-established religious organization that is integrated into the society and does not make strict demands on its members	The belief in spirits capable of helping or harming people
A school program intended to improve the academic performance of socially and educationally disadvantaged children	A collection of beliefs, symbols, and rituals that sanctify the dominant values of a society
The practice of making minorities accept the dominant group's culture	A religious group that professes a new religious belief, totally rejects society, and consists of members with extreme devotion to their leader
The belief in one god	The type of religion that emphasizes moral principles as guides for living a righteous life

Chapter 10 Page 319 Polytheism	Chapter 10 Page 295 Pygmalion Effect
Chapter 10 Page 315 Sect	Chapter 10 Page 321 Shamanism
Chapter 10 Page 319 Theism	Chapter 10 Page 322 Totemism
Chapter 10 Page 294 Tracking	

The impact of a teacher's expectations on student performance	The belief in more than one god
The belief that a spiritual leader can communicate with the spirits by acting as their mouthpiece or letting the soul leave the leader's body and enter the spiritual world	The type of religion that centers on the worship of a god or gods
The belief that a kinship exists between humans and an animal—or, less commonly, a plant	The type of religion that centers on the worship of a god or gods
	The system of sorting students into different groups according to past academic achievement

Chapter 12: The Economy and Politics

Learning Objectives

After reading Chapter 12, the student should be able to:

1. Define the key concepts of the economic institution and politics.
2. Discuss the economy in perspective, including growth of the industrial, capitalist economy, the different sociological perspectives on the economy, and the feminist perspective on women's economic status.
3. Examine aspects of the modern economic system, including capitalism, socialism and economic in the real world.
4. Describe the dominance of big corporations around the world.
5. Describe the different aspects of work in America, and analyze the changing nature of the workplace.
6. Describe the patterns of social diversity in the U.S. economy.
7. Define the nature of power and authority and see how they become expressed in the state.
8. Explore the world of U.S. politics
9. Analyze the question of who really governs using the sociological theories of political power.
10. Undertake a global analysis of political violence.

Key Concepts

alienation of labor
authority
capitalism
charisma
coercion
communism
conglomerate
dual economy
economic institution
ideological conservatives
industrial Revolution
influence
interest grouo

mixed economy
monopoly
multinational corporation
oligopoly
operational liberals
political party
political power
political socialization
politics
postindustrial revolution
power
revolution
socialism
terrorism

Content Select Articles

[Note: The following articles are available to students through ContentSelect, a data base of sociological articles that students can use through purchase of the text. They can be found in the data base by typing in the author's name.]

Title:	Information-Sector Growth in Market and Nonmarket Economies: A Comparative Case Study.
Source:	Information Society, Jul-Sep2001, Vol 17 Issue 3, 5 charts, 10 graphs
Author(s):	Shifflet, Mark
Abstract:	An analysis of the predominant theoretical perspectives on the development of the information society indicates that a comparison of the development of the information workforce in countries that have experienced industrialization under different socioeconomic systems is needed. Finland and Poland have experienced similar patterns.

Title:	Canadian Political Economy's Legacy for Sociology
Source:	Canadian Journal of Sociology, Summer2001, Vol. 26 Issue 3, p405, 16p
Author(s):	Clement, Wallace
Abstract:	Reflects on the emergence of the macrosociological tradition in Canadian Political Economy. Location of the macrosociolgical tradition and its evolution within Canadian scholarship; Presentation of political economy within the discipline of sociology; Definition of political economy in Canada

Title:	Women's Work in the Information Economy: The case of telephone call centers
Source:	Information Communication & Society, Sep2000, Vol. 3 Issue 3, p366, 20p
Author(s):	Belt, Vicki; Richardson, Ranald; Webster, Juliet
Abstract:	This paper is concerned with the work experiences and career opportunities of women employed in technology-intensive offices known as telephone 'call centres'. Call centers have grown rapidly across Europe in recent years, creating a significant number of new jobs and receiving considerable attention within the media, business and academic communities. However, despite the fact that the majority of call centre jobs have been taken by women, researchers have so far paid little attention to their position in this new 'industry'. The article addresses this research gap.

Title:	Superpredidentialism and Political Party Development in Russia, Ukraine, Armenia and Kyrgystan.
Source:	Europe-Asia Studies, Dec2001, Vol. 53 Issue 8, p1177, 15p
Author(s):	Kennedy, Ryan T.
Abstract:	Focuses on the political conditions of several countries comprising the Former Soviet republics. Development of political parties in the countries; Factors that caused the unstable political environment in the countries; Institutional elements that account for the differences among the nations' political party practices.

Title:	Re-Nationalization of Military Strategy?
Source:	Society, Sep/Oct2001, Vol. 53 Issue 6, pg25, 6p

Author(s):   von Bredow, Wilfred
Abstract: Questions the role of the armed forces in international politics.
               Significance of the end of the East-West conflict; Contradiction and
               ambiguities in the promotion of cosmopolitan values in an age of
               globalization; Discussion of the technological changes in the armed
               forces.

Practice Tests

Answers to these questions are found at the end of this manual.

Multiple Choice

_____ 1. Industrialization changes the nature of work by using technology to do the jobs once
         done by people. This causes

   a. an increase in white collar jobs and an increased need for highly educated
       individuals.
   b. severe unemployment.
   c. manufacturing companies to go out of business.
   d. an increase in the need for more blue-collar workers.

_____ 2. Adam Smith believed that capitalism works best when

   a. the government keeps strict control over the economy.
   b. the government adopts a laissez faire policy toward the market.
   c. businesses look to the government for policy standards.
   d. businesses do not establish their own production standard rather than meeting
       consumers' demand.

_____ 3. Functionalists believe that private ownership of businesses

   a. stifles creativity.
   b. motivates people to be productive.
   c. motivates people to contribute more to the less fortunate.
   d. motivates people to sell products at higher prices.

_____ 4. Most Americans were not able to improve their living standards during the 1980s
         because

   a. most American workers lost the work ethic.
   b. Americans purchased too many goods on credit.
   c. the arrival of many immigrants led to the sharing of the same wealth with a larger
       number of persons.
   d. American productivity growth significantly slowed.

_____ 5. Beginning in the 1990s, service industries began to grow rapidly because

    a. there was an increased demand for healthcare, entertainment, and financial services.
    b. there was a demand for more services.
    c. there was a decrease in professional jobs.
    d. there was an increased need for food and clothing.

_____ 6. Membership in unions has continuously been declining since 1983. two reasons for the decline are the loss of unionized manufacturing jobs and the fact that

    a. union fees are too expensive.
    b. service professionals do not have unions.
    c. the union does not appear to well-educated employees.
    d. unions have lost their usefulness.

_____ 7. The ability to control the behavior of others, even against their will, is called

    a. illegitimate power.   c. politics.
    b. influence   d. power

_____ 8. Political parties perform all of the following functions, EXCEPT

    a. recruit candidates and conduct fund raising.
    b. formulate and promote policies.
    c. insure that voters vote for the chosen candidate.
    d. help organize the main institutions of government.

_____ 9. The American political party system

    a. only allows the Republican and Democratic parties to exist.
    b. primarily contains two parties, but other less influential parties exist.
    c. is a three-party system.
    d. has been dominated by Republicans since the Civil War.

_____ 10. Interest groups use all of the following methods in trying to influence governmental policies EXCEPT

    a. they try to influence public opinion.
    b. they endorse sympathetic candidates.
    c. they buy television ads to influence voters.
    d. they file lawsuits to further their goals.

Fill In The Blank

1. _____ is an economic system based on government control and public ownership.

2. _____ do not communicate with each other but have the right to elect a board of directors to operate a company.

3. The process by which people acquire and exercise power and, thereby determine who gets what, when, and how, is called _____.

4. _____ workers are more likely to express satisfaction with their jobs than other workers.

5. Political groups that have the power to block each other's actions are called _____ groups.

True or False

_____ 1. Marx believed that the contradictions of capitalism would lead to a revolution.

_____ 2. The United States and Japan are among the most capitalist societies in the world.

_____ 3. Corporations proportionately pay a larger percentage of income tax than individuals.

_____ 4. Tom's parents are both life-long democrats. Tom will probably vote the democratic line when he reaches legal voting age.

_____ 5. Terrorists are generally powerful individuals who are fighting for a cause.

Essay

1. Identify the four major changes brought about by *industrialization*. How did these changes impact people's way of life?

2. Identify the key characteristics of *capitalism*. How does capitalism lead to a more prosperous economy?

3. Define *dual economy* and describe its three sectors.

4. Identify and describe the conditions required for a *revolution* to occur.

5. Describe how *terrorism* develops and what are its impacts.

Chapter 12 Page 331 Alienation of Labor	Chapter 12 Page 344 Authority
Chapter 12 Page 330 Capitalism	Chapter 12 Page 345 Charisma
Chapter 12 Page 344 Coercion	Chapter 12 Page 331 Communism
Chapter 12 Page 336 Conglomerate	Chapter 12 Page 338 Dual Economy

Legitimate power institutionalized in organizations	Marx's term for laborers' loss of control over their work process
An exceptional personal quality popularly attributed to certain individuals	An economic system based on private ownership of property and competition in producing and selling goods and services
A classless society that operates on the principle of "from each according to his ability to each according to his needs"	The illegitimate use of force or threat of force to compel obedience
An economy that comprises a *core* of giant corporations dominating the market and a *periphery* of small firms competing for the remaining, smaller shares of business	A corporation that owns companies in various unrelated industries

Chapter 12 Page 328 Economic Institution	Chapter 12 Page 347 Ideological Conservatives
Chapter 12 Page 328 Industrial Revolution	Chapter 12 Page 344 Influence
Chapter 12 Page 350 Interest Group	Chapter 12 Page 333 Mixed Economy
Chapter 12 Page 335 Monopoly	Chapter 12 Page 336 Multinational Corporation

U.S. citizens who, in theory, are opposed to big government because of their belief in free enterprise, rugged individualism, and capitalism

A system for producing and distributing goods and services

The ability to control others' behavior through persuasion rather than coercion or authority

The dramatic economic change brought about by the introduction of machines into the work process about 200 years ago

An economic system that contains elements of both capitalism and socialism

An organized collection of people who attempt to influence government policies

Corporations that have subsidiaries in many countries

The situation in which one firm controls the output of an industry

Chapter 12 Page 335 Oligopoly	Chapter 12 Page 347 Operational Liberals
Chapter 12 Page 349 Political Party	Chapter 12 Page 351 Political Power
Chapter 12 Page 346 Political Socialization	Chapter 12 Page 328 Politics
Chapter 12 Page 328 Postindustrial Revolution	Chapter 12 Page 344 Power

U.S. citizens who, in effect, support big government by backing government programs that render services to the public	The situation in which a very few companies control the output of an industry
The capacity to use the government to make decisions that affect the whole society	A group organized for the purpose of gaining government offices
The type of human interaction that involves some people acquiring and exercising power over others	A learning process by which individuals acquire political knowledge, beliefs, and attitudes
The ability to control the behavior of others, even against their will	The change of an economy into one dominated by high technology

Chapter 12 Page 354 Revolution	Chapter 12 Page 331 Socialism
Chapter 12 Page 355 Terrorism	

An economic system based on public ownership and government control of the economy	The movement aimed at the violent overthrow of the existing government
	The use of violence to express dissatisfaction with a government

Chapter 13: Health and Population

Learning Objectives

After reading Chapter 13, the student should be able to:

1. Describe how social forces and health are intertwined, and how sociologists use the field of epidemiology to understand the origins and spread of diseases such as AIDS.
2. Outline characteristics of the medical profession, including the emergence of modern medicine and sexism in medical research, social diversity in seeking medical care, and current aspects of the medical care delivery debate.
3. Understand the functionalist, conflict, and symbolic interactionist perspectives on health care.
4. Describe the global analysis of population, or demography, and describe how the recent U.S Census was conducted.
5. Describe the patterns of population change.
6. List and define methods of combating population growth.
7. Understand the debate surrounding stem cell research as presented in the Sociological Frontiers box, "Societal Reaction to Stem Cell Research."
8. Explore ways of getting medical advise on line as presented in the Using Sociology box, "How to Be a Savvy E-Patient."

Key Concepts

age structure
birth rate
census
death rate
demographic transition
demography
epidemiology
healing role

infant mortality rate
life expectancy
living will
marriage rate
sex ratio
sick role
vital statistics

Content Select Articles

[Note: The following articles are available to students through ContentSelect, a data base of sociological articles that students can use through purchase of the text. They can be found in the data base by typing in the author's name.]

Title: MEDICAL SOCIOLOGY AND PUBLIC HEALTH: PROBLEMS AND PROSPECTS FOR COLLABORATION IN THE NEW MILLENNIUM.

Source: Sociological Spectrum, Jul2001, Vol. 21 Issue 3, p247, 17p

Author(s):   Spitler, Hugh D.

Abstract: Medical sociology and public health share many of the same concerns in the study of social and cultural factors that affect the health of the population. Differences in theoretical approaches, methodological procedures, conceptualization and measurement, and research objectives, however, often serve to limit the potential for collaboration between the two disciplines. Sociologists possess many of the theoretical models and analytical techniques needed in public health for the study of the impact of socioeconomic status, poverty, inequality, differentials in power, and social and cultural differences on disease outcomes and health status.

Title: Globalisation, cultural change and the modern drug epidemic: The case of Hong Kong.

Source: Health, Risk, and Society, Mar2001, Vol 3 Issue 1, 2 charts, 1 graphs

Author(s):   Yi-Mak, Kam; Harrison, Larry

Abstract: This paper focuses on the Hong Kong Special Administrative Region on China, one of the localities in the world where the process of flobalization is most advanced, in order to examine the relationship between globalization and the risk of illicit drug problems. It considers the impact of flobalization on both the supply side and the demabd side of th eillicit drugs market in Hong Kong. It is argued that, historically, the trade in dependence-producing substances like tobacco and opium was central to the creation of a world market; in particular, the nineteenth centry drive to bring Southeast Asia into a system of world trade led to the first of the moder drug 'epidemics'. Hong Kong, ceded to the British following the first Opium War, was central to this project, and to the creation of the financial and tranport infastructure needed to support large-scale opium trading.

Title: Modenization, Gender Equality, and Mortality Rates in Less
              Developed Contries
Source: Sociological Spectrum, Apr-Jun2000, Vol 20. Issue 2, p195, 26p 5
              charst, 1 diagram
Author(s)   Lee, Matthew R.

Abstract: Although greater accessibility tohealth care and increading levels of
              education among residents of less developed contries have clearly
              contributed to mortality decline, few theoretical models to date
              have adequately explained the relationship. A comprehensive
              model of mortality decline should document both the factors that
              directly drive down mortality rates and the underlying sturctual
              dynamics that give rise to such direct effects. The present article
              draws on fundamental diffusion concepts and a psychosociological
              model of modernization that attempts to explain how less
              developed contries increade their avalibility of health care services
              and reduce gender inequality. Two diffusion mechanisms are
              argued to be operating: the transfer of raw material goods and
              technology through the international capitalist exchange system
              and the transfer of modern values, ideas, practives, and knowledge
              through the mass media.

Title: An experimental methodology for estimating Hispanic
              Methodology for Estimating
Source: Journal of Economic & Social Measurement, 1997, Vol 23 Issue 4,
              p263 13p, 3 charts, 1 map
Author(s):   Smith, Stanley K. ; Nogle, June M.

Abstract: Describes and experimental methodology for estimating the
              Hispanic population of states and contries in the United States.
              Data sources used in the study; Estimates of the total Hispanic
              population; Estimates of Hispanic population by age, sex and race;
              Conclusions.

Practice Tests

Answers to these questions are found at the end of this manual.

Multiple Choice

_____ 1. Which of the following statements about the health of U.S. citizens is NOT true?

    a. People in the United States arte much healthier than ever before.
    b. The United States is the healthiest country in the world.
    c. The infant mortality rate has dropped dramatically.
    d. People in nearly all other industrialized countries live longer than those from the U.S.

_____ 2. Women in the U.S. tend to live longer than men because they can survive various illnesses and they

    a. do not work as hard as men.
    b. have better eating habits.
    c. maintain stronger emotional ties with other people.
    d. have illnesses that do not last as long as men.

_____ 3. One reason why epidemiologists collect data about sick persons is to discover

    a. common factors that might locate the cause of the disease.
    b. what is different about the victims of a disease.
    c. how many people currently have a disease.
    d. the personal background of the first and last victim of a disease.

_____ 4. Today, more persons are seeking to become doctors. Which of the following is an important aspect of this new wave of interest?

    a. Numerous students are considerably older than years ago.
    b. More medical students have a greater sense of public duty.
    c. Today's medical students are still overwhelmingly male and come from families with the same backgrounds.
    d. Today's medical students have higher income expectations than ever before.

_____ 5. Many patients in the U.S. die in pain because medial doctors fear retaliation if they use stronger medications. In an effort to assist doctors, medical schools have begun

    a. teaching doctors about the use of strong pain killers.
    b. offering courses on pain medications.
    c. offering courses on assisted-suicide.
    d. offering courses in pain management.

_____ 6. Conflict theorists suggest that the decline of mortality rates for the five infectious diseases during the last century was brought about mostly by

    a. social and environmental factors.
    b. new medical measures.
    c. improved immunizations.
    d. decreased standards of living.

_____ 7. The two factors that shape death rates or life expectancies are medical practice and

    a. immigration.   c. wealth.
    b. health.   d. birthrates.

_____ 8. Which of the following causes of migration is a pull factor?

    a. warmer climate
    b. political oppression or persecution
    c. loss of a job
    d. not enough libraries, museums, or concerts.

_____ 9. The world's population explosion has occurred because

    a. births have increased.
    b. births have decreased.
    c. deaths have increased.
    d. deaths have decreased.

_____ 10. A population can be considered fairly stable when

    a. the birth rate is low and the death rate is high.
    b. the birth rate is high and the death rate is low.
    c. marriage rates and birth rates are stable.
    d. both birth rates and death rates are high.

Fill In The Blank

1. The diseases that hit minority groups the hardest are those associated with _____.

2. Issues of concern about various medical studies have been raised because many of the studies did not include _____.

3. _____ make up the data source for information about a country's births, marriages, and deaths.

4. Conflict theorists suggest that the unequal distribution of health care reflects society's _____.

5. Mandatory sterilization is a form of _____ population control.

True or False

_____ 1. The U.S. Public Health Service has successfully eradicated myths and misconceptions about AIDS.

_____ 2. Most doctors in the U.S. are reluctant to assist suicide because they are trained to save lives.

_____ 3. Malthus argued that population growth could be stopped by medicine.

_____ 4. India and China have abandoned their compulsory population controls in order to increase their populations.

_____ 5. To assist companies in spotting illegal documents often used by illegals to get jobs, the government has established a computer registry for checking social security numbers.

Essay

1. Define *epidemiology* and identify the kinds of data epidemiologists collect and why.

2. Discuss how *living wills* assist people with some issues about health care and dying.

3. Describe the differences between *exponential growth* and *linear growth*.

4. Briefly discuss Thomas Malthus' concepts of *population control*. What was his main idea for controlling population?

5. Define *demographic transition* and describe its four stages.

Chapter 13 Page 382 **Age Structure**	Chapter 13 Page 381 **Birth Rate**
Chapter 13 Page 379 **Census**	Chapter 13 Page 382 **Death Rate**
Chapter 13 Page 384 **Demographic Transition**	Chapter 13 Page 379 **Demography**
Chapter 13 Page 367 **Epidemiology**	Chapter 13 Page 376 **Healing Role**

The number of babies born in a year for every 1,000 members of a given population	The pattern of the proportions of different age groups within a population
The number of deaths in a year for every 1,000 members of a population	A periodic head count of the entire population of a country
The scientific study of population	The theory that human populations tend to go through specific demographic stages and that these stages are tied to a society's economic development
A set of social expectations regarding how a doctor should behave	The study of the origin and spread of disease within a population

Chapter 13 Page 382 Infant Mortality	Chapter 13 Page 382 Life Expectancy
Chapter 13 Page 375 Living Will	Chapter 13 Page 383 Marriage Rate
Chapter 13 Page 383 Sex Ratio	Chapter 13 Page 376 Sick Role
Chapter 13 Page 379 Vital Statistics	

The average number of years that a group of people can expect to live	The number of deaths among infants less than 1 year old for every 1,000 live births
The number of marriages in a given year for every 1,000 people	Advance instructions about what someone wants doctors to do in the event of a terminal illness
A set of social expectations regarding how an ill person should behave	The number of males per 100 females
	Information about births, marriages, deaths, and migrations into and out of a country

Chapter 14: Environment and Urbanization

Learning Objectives

After reading Chapter 14, the student should be able to:

1.   Define ecology and analyze the origins and solutions to the problems of pollution and diminishing resources.
2.   Define "urbanization" and undertake a global analysis of urbanization.
3.   Describe features of cities in the United States.
4.   Explain the idea of urban ecology and describe some urban spatial patterns and ecological processes that shape the urban environment.
5.   Describe the nature of city life.
6.   Analyze the causes of such urban problems as population decline and financial problems.
7.   Describe the three sociological perspectives on urbanization.
8.   Analyze the future of U.S. cities.
9.   Explore the future of U.S. cities as presented in the Sociological Frontiers box, "The Future of U.S. Cities.
10.   Investigate ways of rejuvenating cities as analyzed in the Using Sociology box on "How to Revitalize the City."

Key Concepts

biosphere
compositional theory
concentric zone theory
ecology
ecosystem
empowerment zones
gentrification
megacity
megalopolis

metropolis
multiple-nuclei theory
peripheral theory
sector theory
subcultural theory
urban anomie theory
urban ecological processes
urban ecology
urbanization

Content Select Articles

[Note: The following articles are available to students through ContentSelect, a data base of sociological articles that students can use through purchase of the text. They can be found in the data base by typing in the author's name.]

Title: ENVIRONMENTAL CANCER.
Source: Society, May/Jun2001, Vol. 38 Issue 4, p20, 7p
Author(s):   Rothman, Stanley; Lichter, S. Robert
Abstract: Focuses on issues regarding environmental cancer in the United States (U.S.). Environmental factors that triggered most cancers; Experts' views on the contribution of various aspects of the *environment* to human cancer rates in the U.S.; Environmentalist views on cancer causes.

Title: AT HOME WITH NATURE: Effects of " Greenness" on Children's Cognitive Functioning.
Source: Environment & Behavior, Nov2000, Vol. 32 Issue 6, p775, 21p
Author(s):   Wells, Nancy M.
Abstract: Discusses a study which examined the linkage between the naturalness or restorativeness of the home *environment* and the cognitive functioning of low-income urban children. Restorative effects of the natural *environment*; Theoretical foundation; Method; Results; Discussion.

Title: COALITION FORM AND MOBILIZATION EFFECTIVENESS IN LOCAL SOCIAL MOVEMENTS.
Source: Sociological Spectrum, Apr2001, Vol. 21 Issue 2, p207, 25p, 5 charts
Author(s):   Jones, Andrew W.; Hutchinson, Richard N.; Van Dyke, Nella; Gates, Leslie; Companion, Michele
Abstract: Little has been written on the form that coalitions take in social movements. Three months of fieldwork by a five-person team documented the population of social movement events (SMEs) across seven movements in a Southwestern *city*. We investigated the process and form that led to these events at the interorganizational level. Three different coalition forms, as well as single social movement organizations (SMOs) acting alone, organized the SMEs. The "network invocation" form--a single SMO making strategic and framing decisions while encouraging other SMOs in its network to mobilize participants--was significantly more effective than other forms at mobilizing attendance at events.

Title: Imperial Ghetto: People and Rituals in a South African Ghetto.
Source: Social Identities, Dec2000, Vol. 6 Issue 4, p511, 25p, 22bw
Author(s):   Badsha, Omar
Abstract: Provides photographs on racial spaces and people of the 1980s in the Imperial Ghetto of South Africa. Representation of ghetto history and

development of Durban communities; Racial discrimination in the *city*; Reinterpretations of the past and relationship to North Africa.

Practice Tests

Answers to these questions are found at the end of this manual.

Multiple Choice

_____ 1. Self-sufficient communities of organisms that depend on one another for survival are called _____.

    a. biospheres   c. ecosystems
    b. urban areas   d. ecological areas

_____ 2. The 1990s was the warmest decade on record due to what many scientists call

    a. a heat wave.   c. glacier melts.
    b. global warming.   d. El Nino.

_____ 3. According to the text, two of the causes for pollution and the depletion of resources are

    a. poverty and overuse.
    b. ignorance and waste.
    c. ignorance and poverty.
    d. power plans and coal mines.

_____ 4. Modern technology has increased our impact on the environment indirectly because it

    a. makes us more ignorant about nature.
    b. always creates more pollution.
    c. leads to greater inequality between the rich and the poor.
    d. spurs an increase in wealth and consumption.

_____ 5. Most environmentalists feel that the key to solving the ecological crisis is

    a. totally limiting population growth.
    b. substantially reducing our expectations for consumption.

     c. stopping the development of new technology.
     d. passing new laws.

_____ 6. One of the biggest facilitators in the development of suburbs was the _____.

     a. automobile   c. bus system
     b. commuter trains   d. job market

_____ 7. Today, there are about _____ "megacities," with populations of 5 million or more.

     a. 10   c. 40
     b. 20   d. 80

_____ 8. The latest U.S. Census reveals all of the following changes in American cities over the last decade EXCEPT

     a. cities in the west and south have grown rapidly.
     b. immigration has slowed population decline for some major cities.
     c. most state capitals have increased their population.
     d. minorities have moved out of the inner cities.

_____ 9. _____ emerge in large cities because of the population density and diversity of a city.

     a. communities   c. cultures
     b. suburbs   d. subcultures

_____ 10. Motivated by profit, corporations have helped turn suburbs into "edge cities" by

     a. paying higher taxes.
     b. moving businesses and factories there from central cities.
     c. organizing labor and transportation.
     d. development small city governments.

Fill In The Blank

1. _____ are communities of living things interacting with their environment.

2. _____ ecofeminists attribute environmental problems to capitalism.

3. The population belt extending from Boston to Washington, D.C. or from San Francisco to San Diego is called a (n) _____.

4. _____ may be a factor in housing segregation.

5. Functionalists suggest that the masses of ordinary people are the force behind _____.

True or False

_____ 1. All environmental issues could be solved if people were educated about how to avoid accumulating waste.

_____ 2. One approach to dealing with air pollution is the introduction of a gas-electric car.

_____ 3. Today, the environment is in worse shape than when the first Earth Day was celebrated 30 years ago.

_____ 4. According to the latest U.S. Census, university cities have gained population.

_____ 5. Urban problems stem largely from city government's inability to provide various services to the public.

Essay

1. Define *ecosystem* and identify its principles.

2. Identify and analyze the major causes of *environmental pollution*.

3. Describe how *suburbs* become *edge cities*.

4. Describe the three theories of *spatial patterning* by which many cities are designed. Which pattern do you believe was used to design your hometown?

5. Describe how *subcultures* emerge in cities and the roles they play.

Chapter 14 Page 394 Biosphere	Chapter 14 Page 410 Compositional Theory
Chapter 14 Page 406 Concentric-Zone Theory	Chapter 14 Page 394 Ecology
Chapter 14 Page 394 Ecosystem	Chapter 14 Page 413 Empowerment Zones
Chapter 14 Page 403 Gentrification	Chapter 14 Page 402 Megacity

The theory that city dwellers are as involved with small groups of friends, relatives, and neighbors as are non-city people

A thin layer of air, water, and soil surrounding the earth

A study of the interactions among organisms and between organisms and their physical environment

The model of land use in which the city spreads out from the center in a series of concentric zones, each used for a particular kind of activity

The economically depressed urban areas that businesses, with the help of government grants, low-interest loans, and tax breaks, try to revive by creating jobs; also known as enterprise zones

A self-sufficient community of organisms depending for survival on one another and on the environment

A city with a population of 5 million or more

The movement of affluent people into poor urban neighborhoods

Chapter 14 Page 402 Megalopolis	Chapter 14 Page 401 Metropolis
Chapter 14 Page 408 Multiple-Nuclei Theory	Chapter 14 Page 408 Peripheral Theory
Chapter 14 Page 407 Sector Theory	Chapter 14 Page 411 Subcultural Theory
Chapter 14 Page 409 Urban Anomie Theory	Chapter 14 Page 409 Urban Ecological Processes

A large urban area that includes a city and its surrounding suburbs	A vast area in which many metropolises merge
The model of land use in which suburban cities grow around the central city	The model of land use in which a city is built around many discrete nuclei, each being the center of some specialized activity
The theory that the city enriches people's lives by offering diverse opportunities and developing various subcultures	The model of land use in which a city grows outward in wedge-shaped sectors from the center
Processes in which people compete for certain land use, one group dominates another, and a particular group moves into an area and takes it over from others	The theory that city people have a unique way of life characterized by alienation, impersonal relations, and stress

Chapter 14 Page 406 Urban Ecology	Chapter 14 Page 394 Urbanization

The transformation of rural areas into cities	The study of the relationship between people and their urban environment

Chapter 15: Collective Behavior, Social Movements, and Social Change

Learning Objectives

After reading Chapter 15, the student should be able to:

1.   Understand how the rapid growth of computer technology as seen in the creation of Amazon.com is an important examples of social change.
2.   Define collective behavior and describe its the characteristics and social factors influencing it.
3.   Discuss different forms of collective behavior, including panics, crowds, public opinion and social movements.
4.   Undertake a global analysis of social change, and compare changes in the U.S. to other countries.
5.   Describe the functionalist perspective and the several theories of social change it supports.
6.   Analyze the conflict view of social change.
7.   Detail features of the symbolic interactionist view of change.
8.   Describe some ways the U.S. has changed.
9.   Explore the major changes in the future of American society as analyzed in "Sociological Frontiers: What Our Future Will be Like."
10.   Analyze the safe use of cellphones as presented in "Using Sociology: How to Use Cellphones Properly."

Key Concepts

breakdown-frustration theory
collective behavior
convergence theory
craze
crowd
cyclical theory
divergence theory
emergent norm theory
equilibrium theory
evolutionary theory
fad
fashion
frustration theory
ideational culture

mass hysteria
modernization
opinion leader
panic
principle of immanent change
propaganda
public
public opinion
resource mobilization theory
rumor
sensate culture
social change
social contagion
social movement

Content Select Articles

[Note: The following articles are available to students through ContentSelect, a data base of sociological articles that students can use through purchase of the text. They can be found in the data base by typing in the author's name.]

Title: RETURN OF THE CROWDS AND RATIONALITY OF ACTION: A history of Russian 'financial bubbles' in the mid-1990s.

Source: European Societies, Sep2000, Vol. 2 Issue 3

Author(s): Radaev, Vadim

Abstract: Investigates the models of action of small private investors in the financial bubbles in Russia from 1994 to 1995. Characteristics of data sources and principal method of data analysis; Demonstration of different types of rationality and non-rationality; Information on the main stages of the financial game.

Title: The state and *collective* disorders: The Los Angeles riot...

Source: Social Forces, Dec97, Vol. 76 Issue 2, p357, 21p

Author(s): Useem, Bert

Abstract: Develops a theory of state response to *collective* disorders in Los Angeles, California. Objectives of administrative agencies; Problems related to capacity that must be solve by a public safety agency in response to a *collective* disorder; How government agencies must seek both to be accountable and to maintain administrative capacity.

Title: NEW SOCIAL MOVEMENTS: BETWEEN CIVIL SOCIETY AND COMMUNITARIANISM.

Source: Sociological Spectrum, Jan2002, Vol. 22 Issue 1, p41, 30p

Author(s): Marangudakis, Manussos

Abstract: In an effort to nullify the dehumanizing effects of modern life, New Social Movements (NSMs) tend to snub the principles of civil society and in the process embrace values associated with Rousseau's communitarianism. A crucial precondition for the rise of the latter is the establishment of small and intimate organizations, detached from open and multiple networks. This is an extremely difficult endeavor and few social movements achieve it, since the vast network of only partially overlapping modern institutions dilutes the simplicity and intimacy communitarianism thrives upon. Using ethnographic data from two environmental groups and their efforts to construct communitarian communities, the study suggests that success is based upon the ability of a movement to minimize its links with civil networks.

Title: A Method for Systematically Observing and Recording *Collective* Action.

Source: Sociological Methods & Research, May99, Vol. 27 Issue 4, p451, 48p, 7 diagrams, 1 graph, 1bw

Author(s): Schweingruber, David; McPhail, Clark

Abstract: Describes a set of criteria and procedures for systematically observing and recording *collective* action across temporary gatherings such as political demonstrations. Brief history of *collective behavior* and *collective* action research; Problems in the method for observing *collective* action; Discussion of a revised taxonomy of elementary forms.

Practice Tests

Answers to these questions are found at the end of this manual.

Multiple Choice

_____ 1. Generally, in an unusual or unanticipated situation, norms do not exist to tell people how to behave. As a precondition for panic, this situation is called

    a. mutual facilitation.
    b. lack of cooperation.
    c. emotional facilitation.
    d. lack of emotions.

_____ 2. Traits of a crowd include all of the following EXCEPT

    a. sense of urgency.
    b. communication of mood.
    c. heightened suggestibility.
    d. certainty.

_____ 3. Which of the following is NOT a type of collective behavior?

    a. panic   c. social interaction
    b. fashion   d. a social movement

_____ 4. The idea that everyone drinks COKE is a form of propaganda sociologists call

    a. bandwagon.   c. glittering generality.
    b. card stacking.   d. name calling.

_____ 5. Although fads are basically trivial, they can

    a. lead to powerful new scientific discoveries.
    b. create a sense of innovation and courage.
    c. create a source of status for some people.
    d. change the basic structure of society.

_____ 6. A major criticism of the frustration theory is that it

    a. doesn't explain why reform movements evolve.
    b. doesn't identify a common source of discontent.
    c. blames participants in social movements, rather than society for the frustrations.
    d. blames the government rather than individuals involved in a social movement.

_____ 7. A disaster occurred, and rumors about what happened spread everywhere. Many people turned on their televisions and listened to news accounts of what happened. This example illustrates what gatekeeping role of the media?

    a. the authenticating role   c. the concretizing role
    b. the establishing hierarchy role d. the legitimizing role

_____ 8. According to Paul Kennedy, the failure to solve such social problems in the U.S. as crime, drugs and homelessness

    a. could cause the U.S. to become a world leader.
    b. could increase industrialism.
    c. could cause a tradition to be established.
    d. could cause the U.S. to become a poor developing nation.

_____ 9. According to Eric Hoffer, those who participate in social movements are

    a. idealistic and visionary.
    b. frustrated and troubled.
    c. violent and radical.
    d. upper class and educated.

_____ 10. Joseph Nye and others have criticized Kennedy's argument that the United States is suffering an economic decline, because the U.S.

    a. is a unified, hardworking society.
    b. is a religious country.
    c. continues to be the world's largest economy.
    d. has the world's strongest military power.

Fill In The Blank

1. _____ is collective behavior where numerous people engage in frenzied activity without checking the source of their fear.

2. Social psychologist Gustave LeBon believed that a crowd possessed a _____ mind.

3. _____ movements are seeking only a partial change to society.

4. Sociologist Sorokin called a culture that stresses science as the path to knowledge a _____ culture.

5. Today, more than two-thirds of the U.S. labor force works in _____ industries.

True or False

_____ 1. Sociologists believe rumors to be just a collection of untruths.

_____ 2. Blue jeans are an example of a fashion that did not trickle down to lower status groups.

_____ 3. A craze is a shorter-lived, harmless fad.

_____ 4. Evolutionary, functionalist, cyclical, and conflict theories are all efforts to explain social change in general theoretical terms.

_____ 5. Bill was part of a crowd that became emotional and turned into a violent, crazy-like mob. The emergent-norm theory would most completely explain this example of collective behavior.

Essay

1. Define *collective behavior* and identify its different forms.

2. Define *crowd* and identify its characteristics. Which type of crowd is the most dangerous?

3. Define *rumor* and discuss the factors that contribute to rumors. How easy or how difficult is it to correct rumors?

4. Describe the seven methods used to shape *propaganda*. Which form of propaganda is used by the mass media most often?

5. Describe why the U.S. economy is more prosperous than ever before.

Chapter 15 Page 433 ## Breakdown-Frustration Theory	Chapter 15 Page 422 ## Collective Behavior
Chapter 15 Page 434 ## Convergence Theory	Chapter 15 Page 428 ## Craze
Chapter 15 Page 426 ## Crowd	Chapter 15 Page 436 ## Cyclical Theory
Chapter 15 Page 434 ## Divergence Theory	Chapter 15 Page 428 ## Emergent Norm Theory

Relatively spontaneous, unorganized, and unpredictable social behavior	The theory that a social breakdown can cause a social movement by creating frustration among masses of people
A fad with serious consequences	The theory that modernization will bring the West and non-West together by breaking down cultural barriers to produce a global society
The theory that societies move forward and backward, up and down, in an endless series of cycles	A collection of people temporarily doing something while in proximity to one another
The theory that members of a crowd develop, through interaction, a new norm to deal with the unconventional situation facing them	The theory that emphasizes the growing separation between Western and non-Western cultures

Chapter 15 Page 428 Equilibrium Theory	Chapter 15 Page 436 Evolutionary Theory
Chapter 15 Page 428 Fad	Chapter 15 Page 428 Fashion
Chapter 15 Page 433 Frustration Theory	Chapter 15 Page 437 Ideational Culture
Chapter 15 Page 426 Mass Hysteria	Chapter 15 Page 433 Modernization

The theory that societies change gradually from simple to complex forms

The theory that all the parts of society serve some function and are interdependent

A great though brief enthusiasm among a relatively large number of people for a particular innovation

A temporary enthusiasm for an innovation less respectable than a fashion

Sorokin's term for the culture that emphasizes faith or religion as the key to knowledge and encourages people to value spiritual life

The theory that individuals who participate in social movements are frustrated and troubled

The form of social change that involves the transformation of an agricultural society into an industrial one

A form of collective behavior in which numerous people engage in a frenzied activity without checking the source of their fear

Chapter 15 Page 431 Opinion Leader	Chapter 15 Page 425 Panic
Chapter 15 Page 437 Principle of Immanent Change	Chapter 15 Page 430 Propaganda
Chapter 15 Page 430 Public	Chapter 15 Page 430 Public Opinion
Chapter 15 Page 433 Resource Mobilization	Chapter 15 Page 429 Rumor

A type of collective behavior characterized by a maladaptive, fruitless response to a serious threat	A person whose opinion is respected by others and influences them
Communication tailored to influence opinion	The notion that social change is the product of the social forces that exist within a society
The collection of ideas and attitudes shared by the members of a particular public	A dispersed collection of people who share a particular interest or concern
An unverified story that is spread from one person to another	The theory that social movements result from the availability of resources for mobilization

Chapter 15 Page 437 Sensate Culture	Chapter 15 Page 422 Social Change
Chapter 15 Page 427 Social Contagion	Chapter 15 Page 432 Social Movement

The alteration of society over time	Sorokin's term for the culture that stresses empirical evidence or science as the key to knowledge and urges people to favor a practical, materialistic, and hedonistic way of life
A conscious effort to bring about or prevent change	The spreading of a certain emotion and action from one member of a crowd to another

Practice Test Answers

Chapter 1
The Essence of Sociology

MULTIPLE CHOICE

1. D – See page 5
2. C – See page 9
3. C – See page 10
4. B – See page 11
5. C – See page 9
6. B – See page 12
7. C – See page 13
8. A – See pages 19-20
9. D – See pages 22-23
10. A – See page 25

FILL IN THE BLANK

1. organic solidarity – See page 11
2. outsourcing – See page 4
3. Social marginality – See page 3
4. Addams – See page 10
5. hypothesis – See pages 4-5

TRUE OR FALSE

1. T – See page 9
2. F – See page 10
3. F – See page 11
4. F – See page 13
5. T – See Page 11

ESSAY

1. See pages 7-9
2. See pages 9-10
3. See page 11
4. See pages 13-14
5. See pages 21-22

Chapter 2
SOCIETY AND CULTURE

MULTIPLE CHOICE

1. A – See page 34
2. C – See page 34
3. C – See page 35
4. A – See page 39
5. D – See page 42
6. C – See page 42
7. B – See page 44
8. C – See page 47
9. B – See page 48
10. D – See page 50

FILL IN THE BLANK

1. cultural relativism – See page 82
2. Pop – See page 50
3. role set – See page 34
4. horticultural – see page 36
5. Afrocentrism – See page 50

TRUE OR FALSE

1. T – See page 34
2. F – See page 40
3. T – See page 44
4. F – See page 50
5. F – See page 56

ESSAYS

1. See pages 32-36.
2. See pages 37-39
3. See pages 42-48
4. See pages 43-44
5. See page 56

Chapter 3
SOCIALIZATION

MULTIPLE CHOICE

1. C – See page 66
2. D – See page 66
3. A – See page 68
4. C – See page 75
5. A – See page 81
6. C – See page 81
7. D – See page 82
8. A – See page 82
9. C – See page 84
10. B – See page 88

FILL IN THE BLANK

1. Conventional – See page 72
2. Developmental – See page 84
3. Resocialization – See page 84
4. impersonally – See page 82
5. peer – See page 83

TRUE OR FALSE

1. T – See page 67
2. F – See page 68
3. T – See page 75
4. F – See page 81
5. T – See page 87

ESSAY

1. See pages 66-73
2. See page 73
3. See pages 85-86
4. See pages 86-87
5. See pages 87-88

Chapter 4
SOCIAL INTERACTION IN EVERYDAY LIFE

MULTIPLE CHOICE

1. A – See page 94
2. D – See page 94
3. D – See page 97
4. C – See page 99
5. B – See page 102
6. C – See page 105
7. A – See page 106
8. B – See page 107
9. A – See page 108
10. D – See page 109

FILL IN THE BLANK

1. Exchange – See page 94
2. social – See page 94
3. proxemics – See page 99
4. rituals – See page 106
5. distance – See page 105

TRUE OR FALSE

1. T – See page 96
2. F – See page 97
3. F – See page 102
4. F – See page 111
5. T – See page 111

ESSAY

1. See pages 94-95
2. See pages 100-101
3. See page 106
4. See page 107
5. See pages 109-110

Chapter 5
GROUPS AND ORGANIZATIONS

MULTIPLE CHOICE

1. A – See page 116
2. D – See page 117
3. D – See page 117-118
4. B – See page 120
5. D – See page 119
6. D – See page 125
7. B – See page 127
8. B – See page 128
9. C – See page 130
10. D – See page 134

FILL IN THE BLANK

1. instrumental – See page 119
2. network – See page 123
3. collectivist – See page 129
4. Scientific – See page 127
5. quality – See page 129

TRUE OR FALSE

1. T – See page 117
2. F – See page 120
3. F – See page 125
4. T - See page 128
5. F See page 129

ESSAY

1. See page 117
2. See pages 123-124
3. See pages 127-128
4. See page 130
5. See pages 131 – 134

Chapter 6
DEVIANCE AND CONTROL

MULTIPLE CHOICE

1. D – See page 144
2. C – See page 149
3. A – See page 150
4. C – See page 151
5. B – See page 163
6. C – See page 146
7. B – See page 152
8. C – See page 154
9. A – See page 161
10. D – See page 160

FILL IN THE BLANK

1. Anomie – See page 151
2. innovator – See page 151
3. Phenomenological – See page 157
4. career – See page 157
5. victimless – See page 159

TRUE OR FALSE

1. F – See page 143
2. F - See page 146
3. T – See page 146
4. F – See page 155
5. F – See page 152

ESSAY

1. See page 145
2. See pages 148-149
3. See page 150
4. See page 151
5. See pages 152-153

Chapter 7
THE UNITED STATES AND GLOBAL STRATIFICATION

MULTIPLE CHOICE

1. B – See page 174
2. C – See page 172
3. A – See page 177
4. C – See page 174
5. C – See page 180
6. A – See page 181
7. B – See page 188
8. A – See page 183
9. B – See page 187
10. A – See page 192

FILL IN THE BLANK

1. proletariat – See page 172
2. master-slave – See page 176
3. upper upper – See page 181
4. influx of immigrants – see page 189-190
5. Women – See page 192

TRUE OR FALSE

1. T – See page 176
2. F – See page 181
3. T – See page 183
4. F – See page 186
5. T – See page 191

ESSAY

1. See pages 180-182
2. See pages 185-186
3. See page 198
4. See page 187
5. See pages 187-188

Chapter 8
RACE AND ETHNICITY

MULTIPLE CHOICE

1. B – See page 207
2. C – See page 208
3. D – See page 209
4. A – See page 209
5. C – See page 212
6. A – See page 211
7. D – See page 216
8. B – See page 222
9. B – See page 223
10. C – See page 224

FILL IN THE BLANK

1. pure – See page 207
2. Discrimination – See page 209
3. Asian – see page 216
4. conflict – See page 221
5. Institutionalized – See page 224

TRUE OR FALSE

1. F – See page 217
2. T – See page 218
3. F – See page 209
4. T – See page 221
5. F – See page 225

ESSAY

1. See pages 223-224
2. See pages 209-211
3. See page 221
4. See page 224
5. See page 226

Chapter 9
GENDER AND AGE

MULTIPLE CHOICE

1. D – See page 236
2. A – See page 238
3. B – See page 240
4. B – See page 241
5. A – See page 246
6. C – See page 249
7. B – See page 251
8. D – See page 255
9. A – See page 258
10. C – See page 259

FILL IN THE BLANK

1. Stereotypes – See page 236
2. chromosomes – See page 238
3. men – See page 249
4. Senility – See page 256
5. prejudice – See page 257

TRUE OR FALSE

1. F – See page 236
2. T – See page 238
3. T – See page 241
4. F – See page 256
5. T – See page 259

ESSAY

1. See pages 239-240
2. See page 241
3. See pages 242-243
4. See pages 257-258
5. See page 259

Chapter 10
FAMILIES

MULTIPLE CHOICE

1. B – See page 266
2. D – See page 267
3. D – See page 268
4. C – See page 269
5. C – See pages 268-269
6. A – See page 272
7. C – See page 274
8. B – See page 275
9. A – See page 276
10. A – See page 278

FILL IN THE BLANK

1. arranged – See page 267
2. sexual regulation – See page 268
3. dating – See page 270
4. disapproval – See page 276
5. commitment – See page 282

TRUE OR FALSE

1. F – See page 266
2. T – See page 268
3. F – See pages 268-269
4. T – See page 273
5. F – See page 281

ESSAY

1. See page 267
2. See pages 273-274
3. See pages 274-275
4. See page 282
5. See page 286

Chapter 11
EDUCATION AND RELIGION

MULTIPLE CHOICE

1. C – See page 292
2. B – See page 294
3. C – See page 299
4. D – See page 298
5. A – See page 300
6. B – See page 305
7. D – See page 305
8. A – See page 311-12
9. C – See page 308
10. B – See page 316

FILL IN THE BLANK

1. custodial – See page 293
2. magnet – See page 303
3. identity – See page 306
4. cult – See page 311
5. Theism – See page 319

TRUE OR FALSE

1. F – See page 296
2. F – See page 299
3. T – See page 305
4. T – See page 311
5. F – See page 317

ESSAY

1. See pages 292-294
2. See pages 294-295
3. See page 301
4. See pages 304-306
5. See pages 319-322

Chapter 12
THE ECONOMY AND POLITICS

MULTIPLE CHOICE

1. A – See page 329
2. B – See page 331
3. B - See page 331
4. D – See page 334
5. A – See page 338
6. C – See page 339
7. D – See page 344
8. C – See page 349
9. B – See page 349
10. C – See page 350

FILL IN THE BLANK

1. Socialism – See page 331
2. Stockholders – See page 336
3. politics – See page 328
4. White-collar – See page 339
5. veto – See page 352

TRUE OR FALSE

1. F – See page 331
2. T – See page 333
3. F – See page 336
4. T – See page 346
5. F – See page 356

ESSAY

1. See page 329-330
2. See page 331
3. See pages 338-339
4. See pages 354-55
5. See pages 355-56

Chapter 13
HEALTH AND POPULATION

MULTIPLE CHOICE

1. B – See page 364
2. C – See page 365
3. A – See page 367
4. B – See page 372
5. D – See page 376
6. A – See page 377
7. C – See page 382
8. A – See page 382
9. D – See page 385
10. D – See page 385

FILL IN THE BLANK

1. poverty – See page 366
2. women – See page 373
3. Vital statistics – See page 379
4. inequality – See page 377
5. compulsory – See page 386

TRUE OR FALSE

1. F – See page 369
2. T – See page 375
3. F – See page 383
4. F – See page 386
5. T – See page 388

ESSAY

1. See pages 366-367
2. See page 375
3. See page 380
4. See pages 383-384
5. See pages 384-385

Chapter 14
ENVIRONMENT AND URBANIZATION

MULTIPLE CHOICE

1. C – See page 394
2. B – See page 396
3. C – See page 396
4. D – See page 396
5. B – See page 396
6. A – See page 401
7. C – See page 402
8. D – See page 406
9. D – See page 411
10. B – See page 415

FILL IN THE BLANK

1. Ecosystems – See page 394
2. Socialists – See page 399
3. megalopolis – See page 402
4. Economics – See page 414
5. urbanization – See page 414

TRUE OR FALSE

1. F – See page 396
2. T – See page 398
3. F – See page 398
4. T – See page 406
5. T – See page 412

ESSAY

1. See page 394
2. See pages 395-396
3. See pages 404-405
4. See pages 406-408
5. See page 411

Chapter 15
COLLECTIVE BEHAVIOR, SOCIAL MOVEMENTS, AND SOCIAL CHANGE

MULTIPLE CHOICE

1. B – See page 425
2. D – See page 426
3. C – See pages 428-432
4. A – See page 430
5. C – See page 429
6. C – See page 433
7. A – See page 431
8. D – See page 434
9. B – See page 433
10. C – See page 435

FILL IN THE BLANK

1. Mass hysteria – See page 426
2. collective – See page 427
3. Reform – See page 433
4. sensate – See page 437
5. information services – See page 441

TRUE OR FALSE

1. F – See page 423
2. T – See page 428
3. F – See page 428
4. T – See page 436
5. F – See page 427

ESSAY

1. See pages 422-423
2. See pages 426-427
3. See pages 429-430
4. See page 430
5. See page 440
6.

NOTES

NOTES

NOTES